Praise for *Living Out a Life That Matters*

Paul's last letter, hammered out over a lifetime, contains treasure too often overlooked—but no longer. *Living Out a Life That Matters* combines a doctrinally sound, discovery-style inductive Bible study of 2 Timothy with insightful application and reflection questions to help women fulfill their purpose as devoted Christ-followers. Each lesson focuses on one of Paul's character qualities that he intends to pass on to Timothy, his beloved son in the faith. From their relationship, we learn valuable life lessons. Examples include the importance of mentoring, how to combat false teaching, and how to stand firm in chaos. Sounds like a study fitting for today's challenges—it is. I highly recommend Crickett's new study.

Sue Edwards, Professor Emeritus of Educational Ministries and Leadership, Dallas Theological Seminary and author of the Discover Together Bible study series

There's something beautifully tender about reading someone's final words, and that's exactly what we get to do with Paul in 2 Timothy. Crickett Keeth has given us a gift in this study, inviting us to sit down with Scripture, wrestle with it, and let it transform us. What I love most is how practical it is. Crickett brings Paul's eight qualities to life through everyday situations that actually matter. This study will open your eyes to the extraordinary potential in investing in people and pointing them to Jesus.

Rachel Wojo, author of *Desperate Prayers* and podcaster at *Untangling Prayer*

Crickett Keeth has written a deeply meaningful Bible study that moves beyond theory to transform how Christians live out their faith daily. In this thorough exploration of Paul's letter to Timothy, she equips us with concrete tools to discover our God-given calling, develop our spiritual gifts, and invest in relationships that bear eternal fruit. This outstanding eight-week study will challenge you to actively build a legacy that matters—one encouraging conversation, one faithful act, and one mentored life at a time. I highly recommend it!

Carol Kent, Executive Director of Speak Up Ministries, speaker, and author of *Becoming a Woman of Influence*

I consider Crickett Keeth's study *Living Out a Life That Matters* to be a breath of fresh air in the world of Bible studies for women. Crickett has created questions that allow God's Spirit to move in the lives of women as they study and discuss. The helpful background information provides deeper understanding without giving answers so they can engage the text for themselves. The Leader's Guide equips leaders with practical suggestions for the discussion so that each woman can leave with the main idea and application. I would recommend this study for any small group or church-wide Bible study, knowing that it provides women with a path to grow as disciples of Jesus.

Kay Daigle, Founder of Beyond Ordinary Women Ministries

Crickett Keeth has written a powerful, practical, and deeply biblical study that invites us to live with eternal purpose. *Living Out a Life That Matters* takes us through Paul's final words to Timothy, reminding us that encouragement, faithfulness, strength, and steadfastness are qualities worth pursuing in every season. Whether you're studying alone or with a group, Crickett's questions and reflections will help you dig into Scripture, apply God's truth, and be inspired to invest in the lives of others for His glory. This is a resource I will return to again and again.

Rachael Adams, author of *A Little Goes a Long Way* and host of *The Love Offering* podcast

Crickett Keeth has crafted a Bible study that calls believers to live a life measured not by temporal gain but by eternal fruit—lives shaped by Christ and multiplied through discipleship. I commend this work to all who long to live, not for self, but for the glory of God and the strengthening of His church.

Pace McKee, Senior Pastor of First Evangelical Church, Memphis, TN

Crickett Keeth enthusiastically guides you to plumb the depths of 2 Timothy—Paul's second letter to his faithful disciple. Using probing questions concerning the Scriptures, personal reflections, and prayers, you will progress through this relevant book and emerge encouraged and challenged to be *Living Out a Life That Matters.*

Cynthia Heald, author of the *Becoming a Woman of* . . . Bible study series

In *Living Out a Life That Matters*, Crickett Keeth has created another Bible study suitable for people at all stages of their faith journey. She encourages us to ponder a single, pertinent question: "What is a life that matters?" She then guides us on a journey to find clear, practical answers from Paul's second letter to Timothy. Crickett draws us in with her simple and effective approach to Scripture. She includes solid, succinct summaries of the context. She leads us into our personal growth with reflection questions that stimulate thought. I'm eager to connect with God and His Word through this study!

Neil Tomba, Senior Pastor of Northwest Bible Church in Dallas, TX, and author of *The Listening Road*

Crickett Keeth has written a deeply meaningful eight-week study that calls us to live with purpose and finish well. In *Living Out a Life That Matters*, she beautifully weaves Paul's wisdom to Timothy into practical encouragement for today's believer. Each week points us toward a life of faithfulness, courage, and steadfast devotion to Christ. Crickett's heart for investing in others shines through every page—this is a study that both challenges and refreshes the soul.

Maggie Wallem Rowe, speaker and author of *This Life We Share*

Crickett loves people, and she loves Jesus. In *Living Out a Life That Matters*, Crickett skillfully guides us into ancient wisdom, personal reflection, and practical, present-day application. This study is a master class in studying the Scriptures. My life has been challenged and deepened as I have spent time with Jesus in 2 Timothy . . . with Crickett.

Holly Sheldon, Global Vice President, Student-Led Movements, Campus Crusade for Christ International/Cru

AN 8-WEEK STUDY *in* 2 TIMOTHY

Living Out a Life *That* Matters

CRICKETT KEETH

MOODY PUBLISHERS
CHICAGO

© 2026 by
Crickett Keeth

All rights reserved. No part of this book may be reproduced in any form without permission in writing from the publisher, except in the case of brief quotations embodied in critical articles or reviews. No part of this book may be used as part of a prompt or training for AI software without permission in writing from the publisher.

All Scripture quotations, unless otherwise indicated, are taken from the (NASB®) New American Standard Bible®, Copyright © 1960, 1971, 1977, 1995, 2020 by The Lockman Foundation. Used by permission. All rights reserved. www.Lockman.org

Scripture quotations marked (NLT) are taken from the Holy Bible, New Living Translation, copyright ©1996, 2004, 2015 by Tyndale House Foundation. Used by permission of Tyndale House Publishers, Carol Stream, Illinois 60188. All rights reserved.

All emphasis in Scripture has been added.

Represented by Cynthia Ruchti of Books and Such Literary Agency.

Edited by Amanda Cleary Eastep

Interior design: Puckett Smartt
Cover design: Koko Toyama
Cover graphics of gold brushstrokes copyright © 2025 by Lisima/Creative Market. All rights reserved.
Author photo: Nancy B. Webb Photography

ISBN: 978-0-8024-3757-0

Originally delivered by fleets of horse-drawn wagons, the affordable paperbacks from D. L. Moody's publishing house resourced the church and served everyday people. Now, after more than 125 years of publishing and ministry, Moody Publishers' mission remains the same—even if our delivery systems have changed a bit. For more information on other books (and resources) created from a biblical perspective, go to www.moodypublishers.com or write to:

Moody Publishers
820 N. LaSalle Boulevard
Chicago, IL 60610

1 3 5 7 9 10 8 6 4 2

Printed in the United States of America

This Bible study is dedicated to Bonnie James DeArmond.
She walked into my dorm room one Friday afternoon when I was a junior at Louisiana State University and changed my life.
Even though I was a Christian, I had put God in the "back seat" and was making choices apart from His leading. Bonnie helped me surrender all to the Lord Jesus Christ, and my life hasn't been the same since.
She discipled and helped ground me in my faith. She demonstrated how to disciple others—not just with her words, but also through her actions.

Bonnie, you are a true example of someone living a life that matters.
Thank you for investing in my life and equipping me to make a difference in the lives of others.

CONTENTS

What Is a Life That Matters?

What comes to mind when you hear the phrase, *a life that matters*?

- Financial wealth?
- Material possessions?
- Great achievements?

It is so much more than that. The best investment we can make during our time on earth, in addition to our own spiritual health, is investing in the lives of others. But what does that look like? How do we spur others on to become all God created them to be? How do we live a life worth emulating and one that continues to have an impact long after we're gone?

To help answer these questions, we'll look at the life of the apostle Paul in the book of 2 Timothy. In each week of this eight-week Bible study, we will address one of the qualities Paul modeled to help his young friend Timothy fulfill his God-given purpose and make a difference:

- Encouragement
- Faithfulness
- Strength
- Diligence
- Vigilance
- Equipping
- Commitment
- Steadfastness

Paul recognized the importance of investing in the lives of others, helping them grow in their faith and preparing them to carry out God's purpose. Timothy was one of those Paul chose to equip for carrying on the Lord's work after he was gone, and this young man became a leader in the Ephesian church.

Paul first met Timothy in Lystra on his second missionary journey (Acts 16:1–3), where he recruited Timothy to join him on his travels. It's unclear whether Paul led Timothy to the Lord or if he was already a believer, led to Christ by the influence of his godly mother and grandmother. Regardless, Paul discipled and mentored this young man, helping him develop his gifts and ministry and grow in his relationship with Christ. He often referred to Timothy as his beloved son.

During Paul's final years, persecution against Christians increased under Nero's rule. Paul wrote two pastoral letters to Timothy during this time to guide and encourage him in Ephesus. The purpose of Paul's first letter was to instruct him in the conduct and organization of the church. This second letter was written to direct him as he dealt with false teaching and to spur him on to stand firm in difficult times.

Paul made a difference with his life as he prepared Timothy and others to continue the ministry he was entrusting to them. He left a legacy of eternal significance.

As you study 2 Timothy, I pray you will follow Paul's example by living out these eight qualities in your daily life, while cultivating them in your children, grandchildren, nieces and nephews, friends, and neighbors, whether you're meeting together casually or in a formal mentoring/discipleship relationship. You can make a difference as you demonstrate Christ through these qualities, pointing others to the Lord and helping them become more like Him.

How to Make the Most of This Study

As you journey through this study, allow God to teach you from His Word. Rather than providing extensive commentary or answers to the questions directly following the prompts, I've formatted the study so that you'll need to dig into the Word on your own.

Some questions will be easy as you're asked to write down observations about the passage. But there will also be questions that go beyond simple answers—questions that will challenge and make you ponder what the original author meant. Don't get discouraged if you're not sure how to answer. The purpose of those questions is to move you to a deeper study of the passage and promote rich discussion in small groups. With the more challenging questions, try to answer them on your own first before looking at a commentary, study Bible, or the Leader's Guide in the back of this book.

Each week's lesson provides five days of study. Each day contains four sections:

Looking to God's Word directs you to the Scripture reading for that day, guiding you through observation and interpretation questions.

Looking Upward challenges you to wrestle with thought-provoking questions on your own or in group discussion.

Looking Deeper encourages you to look at additional passages that will give helpful insight into the passage for that day.

Looking Reflectively focuses on reflection of the lesson and personal application.

To get the most out of this study, take time each day to complete a lesson and reflect on the passage and main thought(s), allowing God to speak to you and work in you through His Word. Each week we'll memorize a verse from 2 Timothy.

You can listen to the recordings or watch the videos of the lectures from this study for free on my website at **https://www.crickettkeeth.com/teaching/**.

WEEK ONE

Encouragement

Imagine the emotions Paul must have experienced as he penned his final letter to Timothy, a young man into whom he had poured his life. Paul probably felt a mixture of sadness and joy: sadness that this could be his final letter to Timothy before he left this earthly home, and joy in knowing Timothy was ready to take the baton and continue the ministry Paul had been preparing him for. Paul had modeled a life that matters as he poured into Timothy. Now he exhorts Timothy to follow his example.

When Paul wrote his final words in this letter, he was in prison and believed he would finish his remaining time on this earth behind bars. Paul had seen Timothy's strengths and weaknesses and encouraged him to use his gifts to serve God and live out his purpose. He wanted to make a difference for eternity in the lives of Timothy and others. As he invested in these men, he demonstrated how we, too, can have a positive influence on those God has placed in our lives.

Memory Verse: 2 Timothy 1:7. Write it below.

DAY ONE

Overview of the Letter

Paul wrote this letter to Timothy from prison in Rome. Unlike the first time when he was under house arrest in Rome, this time he was in a dark, lonely cell. Emperor Nero imprisoned Paul in AD 66–67. Most scholars believe he most likely wrote this letter in the fall of AD 67. A few months later, according to tradition, Paul was beheaded outside Rome shortly before Nero's suicide in June of AD 68.[1] This was a difficult time for Christians, and some were hesitant about sharing the gospel or meeting with other believers for fear of what might happen to them. Paul knew he would soon leave his earthly home, and he wanted to encourage Timothy in his ministry during these challenging days.

In this week's lesson, we'll get an overview of how Paul encouraged Timothy by loving him, praying for him, affirming him, exhorting him, and reminding him of God's available resources for growing more like Christ and honoring Him. Let's learn from Paul's life.

Father, thank You for the ones You've placed in my life
who have challenged me to press on in my walk with You.
Thank You for those You've given me to encourage and come alongside.
Help me keep my eyes fixed on You and point others to You.

Looking to God's Word

Read the entire letter of 2 Timothy in one sitting to get an overview.

1. *What is the overall tone and mood of the letter?*

2. *What does Paul want to convey to Timothy?*

3. *What words and ideas are repeated throughout the letter? Why do you think Paul emphasized these things?*

4. *List key people mentioned and write down anything you learn about them.*

Looking Upward

5. If you were the recipient of this letter, what emotions would you be feeling?

Looking Deeper

6. What key verses stand out to you from this letter and why?

Looking Reflectively

A high school or college commencement address isn't a "now that it's over" but a "now that it's beginning" speech. That may have been the thought in Paul's mind—what lies ahead—as he spoke his final words of encouragement and instruction to his student Timothy. Paul had a special relationship with this young man and wanted him to live his life for the Lord. Although his words in this letter were to Timothy, they are also relevant for us today.

✦ *What is one thing (or more) you want to apply from Paul's words?*

"In this last letter, brimming with quiet emotion, Paul reflected on his life and encouraged, warned, instructed, and exhorted Timothy. It's as though Paul were saying, 'I'm trusting you to carry on, Timothy. Stay faithful, stay strong, watch out, and take care!'"[2]

—Bruce Barton et al.

DAY TWO

Encouragement Through Words of Greeting

When I returned home after living in East Asia for four years, I found a sign on my bed where Mom had handwritten a greeting on a poster board: *Welcome home, my darling. It's so good to have you home again. We love you!* Seeing that sign made me smile and cry at the same time, in a good way. Those words made me feel loved and valued, and I took a picture to keep with me as a sweet reminder.

How do we encourage others with our words—written and spoken? We may not send handwritten letters or notes as often anymore. Instead, we email or text when we want to communicate. In handwritten messages, we typically begin our correspondence by addressing the recipient(s). Paul began his letters this way, as well as stating up front that the letter was from him. He began with words of encouragement. Today we'll focus on the salutation and greeting that begins Paul's letter.

Father, thank You for giving me a glimpse into Paul's relationship with Timothy. Help me follow his example in reaching out to those You've put in my life. Show me how to encourage others the way Paul encouraged Timothy.

Looking to God's Word

2 Timothy 1:1–2

1. *How is the salutation in this second letter similar to the salutation in his first letter (1 Tim. 1:1–2)? How do they differ? (For your convenience, I've written them out for you below. You may want to underline what's similar and circle what's different.)*

   1 Timothy 1:1–2
   "Paul, an apostle of Christ Jesus according to the commandment of God our Savior, and of Christ Jesus, who is our hope, To Timothy, my true son in the faith: Grace, mercy, and peace from God the Father and Christ Jesus our Lord."

   2 Timothy 1:1–2
   "Paul, an apostle of Christ Jesus by the will of God, according to the promise of life in Christ Jesus, To Timothy, my beloved son: Grace, mercy, and peace from God the Father and Christ Jesus our Lord."

2. *What do you learn about Timothy in the above greetings? Look up 1 Corinthians 4:17. What else do you learn?*

3. *How does Paul describe himself in 2 Timothy 1:1? Why do you think he identified himself this way?*

John MacArthur explained "apostle" in this way: "*Apostolos* (**apostle**) literally means one who is sent out, 'a messenger,' as it is sometimes translated. . . . But in the New Testament it more commonly carries the connotation of ambassador, a representative who carries with him the authority of the one he represents."[3]

4. Who else did Paul refer to as a messenger in the verses below? How did he describe them?

2 Corinthians 8:23

"As for Titus, he is my partner and fellow worker among you; as for our brothers, they are messengers of the churches, a glory to Christ."

Philippians 2:25

"But I thought it necessary to send to you Epaphroditus, my brother and fellow worker and fellow soldier, who is also your messenger and minister to my need."

5. Paul states he is an apostle of Christ Jesus by the will of God. Why is that significant?

6. What does he mean by the phrase "according to the promise of life in Christ Jesus"?

Looking Upward

7. *Paul used his customary greeting: "Grace, mercy, and peace from God the Father and Christ Jesus our Lord." How would you define grace, mercy, and peace? How are they related? How do they differ?*

8. *How do these words encourage you?*

Looking Deeper

9. *Paul was an encourager to all around him. Read Philemon, verses 4–7. How did Paul affirm and encourage Philemon with his words in this letter (epistle) to Philemon?*

Looking Reflectively

Words of affirmation can go a long way in encouraging someone.

"I believe in you."
"You've got this."
"Great job."

Those words give a bounce in our step and confidence to move forward. We all face moments when we feel unworthy or inadequate, afraid to step out of our comfort zone. Will we be sensitive to those around us who need a word of encouragement? Perhaps our words of greeting and confidence will be exactly what they need at that specific time.

Paul was Timothy's spiritual father and wanted to help him grow in his faith and ministry. We'd be wise to follow Paul's example with those God places in our lives.

✦ *Who is your "Timothy"? Is there someone you are coming alongside to help grow in their relationship with Christ?*

This could be a child, family member, neighbor, or coworker. Perhaps it's a young believer who has questions about their new faith and needs direction. It could be a friend who's struggling with their faith or questioning God. Maybe it's someone dealing with a personal struggle or illness, or a young person who's got questions about life or the Bible. It may be a new mom or newlywed desiring to be the best mom or wife they can be.

✦ *How are you encouraging them? Through Bible study, talking through a situation, praying together, helping with a need, discussing a book, or something else? Take a moment to pray for them now.*

If you aren't in an ongoing relationship in which you disciple or mentor, ask God to show you someone you can speak words of encouragement to.

"A natural leader by any measure, Paul became a great spiritual leader when his heart and mind were captured by Jesus Christ. Paul had boundless, Christ-centered ambition. His supreme love for Christ coupled with the obligation to share Christ's message were his powerful lifetime motives."[4]

—J. Oswald Sanders

DAY THREE

Encouragement Through Relationships

It's hard to imagine life without relationships—laughing and crying together, helping in difficult times, affirming one another, sharing feelings, and simply having fun. Paul and Timothy had a special friendship, and Paul made sure Timothy knew how he felt about him.

Think of all the different relationships in your life—family, friends, coworkers, neighbors, or acquaintances. How have those relationships encouraged you? God brings people into our lives for a reason, and sometimes only for a season. Embrace that time together. Encourage them with your words and actions.

Father, thank You for the relationships You've brought into my life to help me grow in my walk with You. I also thank You for those who have challenged me and the way You have used them to deepen my dependence on You. Keep me mindful that You don't want us to do life alone, but in community.

Looking to God's Word

2 Timothy 1:3–4

1. *Describe Paul's relationship with Timothy. What emotions does he express as he remembers Timothy?*

2. *Paul stated in verse 3 that he served God with a "clear conscience." What do you think that means? What leads to a clear conscience?*

3. *What additional insight do these verses below give concerning a clear conscience?*

   Acts 23:1

   Acts 24:16

1 Timothy 1:5

Hebrews 10:19–22

4. Who are the "forefathers" Paul referred to in 2 Timothy 1:3?

Looking Upward

5. If someone asked you why you serve Jesus Christ, how would you answer that question? What is your motivation?

6. Paul prayed faithfully and consistently for Timothy. What helps you be consistent and faithful in praying for others? What hinders you?

Looking Deeper

7. Review Timothy's background in Acts 16:1–5. What do you learn about him in this passage?

Looking Reflectively

Timothy was not only a spiritual child to Paul, but also a dear friend. Paul encouraged Timothy by praying for him, exhorting him, and equipping him for his ministry. We need people like that in our lives, and I want to be that person for others.

I'm so thankful for the women who have discipled me over the years. They loved me, prayed for and with me, taught me how to share the gospel and study the Bible, and equipped me to carry out the ministry to which God called me. I recently reunited with Bonnie, the first woman to disciple me at Louisiana State University, after thirty-five years. What a joy it was to hug her and tell her face-to-face the difference she made in my life.

✦ *Who are some people who have made a difference in your life for good? Perhaps a teacher, a Sunday school teacher, a friend, or a family member? How did they encourage and help you? (It could be an area of life you were struggling with or your spiritual growth.) Spend time thanking God for them.*

✦ *Be available for God to use you in someone's life. Ask Him to show you opportunities to encourage someone today with your words and actions.*

"A little word of encouragement offered at the right moment can be the difference between finishing well and collapsing along the way, can't it? In our everyday lives, simple heartfelt words can make such a significant impact on our strength and ability to carry on."[5]

—Rachael Adams

DAY FOUR

Encouragement Through Affirmation

My parents and my grandmother (Mamaw) taught me from an early age about Jesus and what He did for me. They helped me understand that I needed to put my faith in Jesus as my Savior to pay the penalty for my sins and not rely on my works to get into heaven. As a result, I came to Christ at the age of nine, and they set examples for how to walk with God. Daddy would read to me from his big black Bible every night as I sat in his lap. Mamaw taught me how to pray and memorize Scripture. And Mom demonstrated what it looked like to walk with Christ intimately, especially in challenging times. They helped shape my life.

Who are the people who have played a role in your spiritual growth? Who has helped you grow in your faith? Today, we'll focus on Timothy's spiritual heritage and how Paul exhorted him to stay strong in his faith.

Father, thank You for those who have
helped me come to know You and grow in my faith.
Make me attentive to those You place in my life whom I can walk
alongside and help develop a deeper relationship with You.
Help me be an affirming spiritual mother and friend.

Looking to God's Word

2 Timothy 1:5–6

1. *What was Timothy's godly heritage? Who influenced him spiritually?*

2. *How did Paul affirm Timothy in these verses?*

3. *Verse 6 begins, "For this reason." To what was Paul referring?*

4. *What is the "gift of God" that Paul mentioned in verse 6? Read 1 Timothy 4:12–14 for additional insight. (Also, I address this in more detail in the Leader's Guide.)*

5. *Paul reminded Timothy to "kindle afresh the gift of God." What do you think that means? How would someone go about doing this?*

6. What are some possible reasons why Paul would need to remind Timothy of this? (You may want to review the introduction for the setting of this letter.)

Looking Upward

7. Do you know what your spiritual gifts are? How do we determine what they are?

To help guide you in this process, read 1 Peter 4:10–11. Peter points out that there are serving gifts and speaking gifts. The serving gifts carry out the ministry of practical service—helps, encouragement, giving, mercy, hospitality, administration. The speaking gifts carry out the ministry of the Word—teaching, exhortation, prophecy (speaking the truth of God's Word), evangelism. Both ministries are essential. You may have both a speaking gift and a serving gift, but usually your gifts are more aligned with one of these two areas.

8. Are your spiritual gifts in speaking or serving? Which area are you most comfortable in and excited about? What are some practical ways you can develop and use those gifts? (For more information on gifts, see the passages below in the Looking Deeper section.)

Looking Deeper

9. There are several passages that list spiritual gifts, but no one passage is comprehensive in listing all of them. Read the Scriptures below and list the gifts mentioned in each. Mark any you think might be your spiritual gifts.

Romans 12:6–8

1 Corinthians 12:4–11, 28

Ephesians 4:11–13

Looking Reflectively

On several occasions, I wanted to quit writing Bible studies. I vividly remember my first rejection of a book proposal sent to a publisher. As my small group Bible study huddled around me to pray, I cried to God, *Lord, I thought this was what You wanted me to do, but I'm obviously no good at it.* My friends, however, affirmed and encouraged me to keep writing as they shared how God had used my words to deepen their walk with God. I'm so thankful for words of affirmation from friends who wouldn't let me quit when I was overwhelmed with doubt and discouragement.

We don't know exactly what was going on with Timothy at the time, but Paul affirmed and exhorted him to keep going and "kindle afresh the gift of God." He reminded Timothy of his godly heritage through his mother and grandmother. Paul was also part of Timothy's spiritual heritage and wanted him to live out his God-given purpose. We all need encouragers in the faith who will spur us on and not let us lose our zeal for God and His work. And we need to be an encourager to others.

✦ *How would you recognize if you need to "kindle afresh the gift of God which is in you"?*

✦ *Use Paul's prayer in 2 Thessalonians 1:11–12 to guide you through praying for someone who needs encouragement and affirmation today.*

> *"The heritage of genuine faith and the special relationships through which it was transmitted to Timothy were recalled to restore his confidence. But they also called to mind a responsibility (to continue in the faith, to persevere in ministry) that he could not walk away from. No matter how bitter the opposition, he could not deny his heritage."*[6]
>
> —Philip Towner

DAY FIVE

Encouragement Through Exhortation

The first time I led a Bible study in college, I was terrified! Doubts flooded my mind, and I told the girl discipling me, "I can't do it." Thankfully, she encouraged me to step out in faith and trust God to work through me even though I felt inadequate. Was it perfect? No. However, I learned much through that experience that continues to spur me on today. I'm thankful someone believed in me and lovingly exhorted me to develop my spiritual gifts.

We all have times when we feel inadequate and weak, but God promises to give us everything necessary to accomplish what He calls us to do. In those times, God enables us as we draw near to Him and draw from His strength, not our own. He brings us into a deeper dependence on Him. Sometimes, we need someone to "push" us to step out in faith and follow God's leading, being confident that God will be sufficient. Paul did that with Timothy.

Father, thank You that I don't have to walk the Christian life on my own strength. You provide the resources to obey and carry out the work You've given me to do. Thank You for enabling me to do Your will each day.

Looking to God's Word

2 Timothy 1:7

1. *Write out 2 Timothy 1:7 below. What contrast does Paul make?*

2. *What does a spirit of timidity look like in ministry?*

3. *God has given us a spirit of power. What does that look like in a believer's life?*

4. *God has also given us a spirit of love. How can we demonstrate a spirit of love?*

5. *God has given us a spirit of discipline. This can also be translated as self-discipline, self-control, or a sound mind. What does that mean to you?*

6. Paul had told Timothy to "discipline yourself for the purpose of godliness" in 1 Timothy 4:7. What does that look like in our lives?

Looking Upward

7. Why are these three qualities—power, love, and discipline—important for those who want to serve God and minister to others?

Looking Deeper

8. God has given us a spirit of power. Is this referring to our own strength or something else? What additional insight do these verses give?

Acts 1:8

1 Corinthians 2:3–5

2 Corinthians 3:4–5

Looking Reflectively

At times, I've let a spirit of timidity overwhelm me. When I was offered the position as the women's ministry director at a church in Memphis, my first response was one of fear. I had not served in that role before. *What if I fail? What if I disappoint them? What if they don't like me?* I felt inadequate and inferior, so I hesitated to say yes. Thankfully, I had some "Paulettes" in my life who wouldn't let me give in to those fears, and they urged me to step out in faith and follow God's leading. I'm so glad they did. God doesn't want us to live in fear of what might happen or what people might think. He wants us to live boldly for Him as He gives us all the resources necessary to do that—in His strength, not our own. His strength is sufficient for any task to which He calls us.

Paul was a great encourager. He was committed to a ministry of encouragement to his disciples and children in the faith, and he spurred them on to be all God intended for them to be. It's fitting that he began this letter to Timothy with words of encouragement.

✦ *Take some time to reflect on today's verse. How can you grow in these four areas?*

Boldness, not timidity

Power

Love

Discipline

✦ *As you reflect on this week's theme of encouragement, how are you encouraging others with your words and actions? How can you strengthen your ministry of encouragement?*

"If you sense that God is calling you to do something far beyond your natural capabilities, you can take heart from Timothy's life. In truth, God always calls us to minister beyond our natural endowments, no matter how great they are.

Take heart! God's call is always too great for us to do in ourselves. But if he calls you, he will equip and enable you to do it."[7]

—R. Kent Hughes and Bryan Chapell

WEEK TWO

Faithfulness

What comes to mind when you hear the word *faithfulness*? Perhaps you think of marriage vows, work commitments, or friendships. I think of people who are true to their word and keep their promises. Faithfulness is a powerful quality, but most of us have probably suffered from someone's unfaithfulness, or we've hurt others by not being true to our word.

Our God is faithful and will always keep His promises. He will never fail us, even when He seems silent or we don't understand what He's doing at the time. As we become more like Him, faithfulness should be evident in our lives.

In the previous passage, Paul reminded Timothy of his spiritual heritage and all that God had given him to accomplish in ministry. Now he challenged Timothy to remain faithful to his calling, knowing he would face tough times ahead.

Be faithful—no matter how hard times get, no matter how inadequate you feel, no matter what others may say. Be faithful to what God has called you to do.

Memory Verse: 2 Timothy 1:14. Write it below.

DAY ONE

Be Faithful to Suffer Well

The Christian life isn't easy. Yes, there will be times when everything goes smoothly, and you're on top of the world. However, there will also be seasons when life is hard, and you find yourself in the middle of a challenging relationship, a financial hardship, a dreaded diagnosis, a deep loss, or suffering for the sake of the gospel. Will you be faithful to suffer well? Will you be faithful to God regardless of your circumstances?

Paul encouraged Timothy to suffer well and trust in God. Be faithful—be full of faith. Let's embrace this exhortation in our own lives.

Father, thank You for Your faithfulness. Help me develop that quality in my walk with You, especially in times of suffering. Keep me true to my word. Convict me, Lord, when I'm not faithful. I desire to please You.

Looking to God's Word

2 Timothy 1:8

1. *When we see a "therefore," we need to look at the preceding context to help us understand what he's about to say. How does this verse relate to what Paul had just stated?*

2. *What are the two things Paul exhorted Timothy not to be ashamed of? What did Paul exhort him to do instead?*

3. *What do you think Paul meant when he referred to himself as "His prisoner"?*

4. *Paul didn't ask Timothy to do anything he wasn't willing to do himself. What insight does Romans 1:16 give concerning why Paul was not ashamed of the gospel?*

5. *What does it mean to be ashamed of the testimony of our Lord? What actions would demonstrate that we're ashamed of the gospel?*

Looking Upward

6. *Paul challenges Timothy to join with him in suffering for the gospel. We may not experience imprisonment for following Christ, but what are some ways we can personally join in the suffering for the gospel of Jesus Christ today?*

Looking Deeper

7. *Read Matthew 26:33–35 and Matthew 26:69–75. What principles can we apply from Peter's fear of the consequences of being associated with Christ? How did he handle his fear? How could he have handled it differently?*

Looking Reflectively

Many of us know Christians who are suffering for their faith in other parts of the world. I asked a young man who's involved in a ministry in a country where the persecution of Christians is on the rise if he was going to stop sharing Christ during this time. His answer was, "No! I will continue to share the gospel and trust God with whatever happens, but I will not be quiet."

A Christian friend from another country asked us not to pray that God would remove the persecution, but that God would give them boldness to witness and wisdom to respond in a way that glorifies God. Will we be able to respond in this way if and when that time comes for us? *Lord, help us be faithful in whatever circumstances we may face.*

✦ *How have you suffered for the gospel? How did you respond?*

✦ *Write out 2 Timothy 1:8 in your own words, making it a prayer to the Lord.*

"God's goal isn't to make us comfortable here but to help us know Him and to intensify our longings for Him. Our troubles are not signs of abandonment but are evidence that He is mightily at work. He uses trouble to draw us closer and open our eyes to see more of Him."[1]

—Carolyn Custis James

DAY TWO

Be Faithful to Your Calling

We each have a calling from God, and He has gifted and shaped us to carry out that purpose. I am most fulfilled when investing my time in areas for which God has designed me. Living out my calling energizes me, but I'm weary and restless when doing tasks God didn't intend for me to do. A great way we can invest in others is to help them discover their gifts and natural abilities and encourage them to use those gifts for God's glory. However, before we can encourage someone else to be faithful to their calling from God, we must first set an example by being faithful to our own calling.

We looked at verse 8 yesterday, which is the beginning of a lengthy sentence that continues in verses 9–11. Today we'll focus on the complete sentence. Ask God to teach you through Paul's words about your calling.

Father, thank You for uniquely designing me for Your specific purpose.
I desire to use those gifts and abilities to fulfill Your calling and not waste them.
Use me to help others discover and use their gifts for Your glory.
Thank You for inviting me to be part of Your greater work
through my God-given calling. I love You, Lord.

Looking to God's Word

2 Timothy 1:8–11

1. *What are the two things God has done concerning us in verse 9? How do they relate to one another?*

2. *How did He accomplish those two things?*

3. *What do you learn about Jesus and our calling in these verses?*

4. *Write down anything else that stands out from this passage.*

5. *What was Paul's calling from God (v. 11)? (See also 1 Tim. 2:7.)*

Looking Upward

6. Paul knew his God-given calling. How do you determine what your calling is? (We'll look closer at this below in Looking Reflectively and again in Week 7.)

7. What do you think God has called you to do?

Looking Deeper

8. How do Paul's words in the passages below support what he's telling Timothy about his salvation and calling?

Ephesians 2:8–10

"For by grace you have been saved through faith; and this is not of yourselves, it is the gift of God; not a result of works, so that no one may boast. For we are His workmanship, created in Christ Jesus for good works, which God prepared beforehand so that we would walk in them."

Titus 3:4–7

"But when the kindness of God our Savior and His love for mankind appeared, He saved us, not on the basis of deeds which we did in righteousness, but in accordance with His mercy, by the washing of regeneration and renewing by the Holy Spirit, whom He richly poured out upon us through Jesus Christ our Savior, so that being justified by His grace we would be made heirs according to the hope of eternal life."

Looking Reflectively

When I'm asked to teach God's Word, I get excited and energized. But when someone asks me to head up a reception with food and decorations, I panic. I'm not gifted in that area, but many around me love using their gifts of service and hospitality for that purpose. Knowing our calling from God helps us discern what to say no to—those tasks that would drain us and take time away from His plan for our lives. Knowing our calling also guides us in what to say yes to and how to invest our time and gifts.

Paul knew what God had called him to do during his time on this earth. God had a purpose for him, but Paul didn't boast about his strengths or focus on himself. His focus was on God, and there is humility in Paul's words. What a great model and reminder for us. God has gifted us for His purpose, and as we carry out that mission, the glory goes to God and Him alone.

One of my greatest joys is helping women discover their God-given calling. Begin by identifying your spiritual gifts. Try serving in different areas to see what is a good fit and what isn't. It's also helpful to ask those who know you well what they think your spiritual gifts are.

Then consider these questions:

- *What do you enjoy doing? What energizes you? What are you passionate about?*

- *What are you naturally good at? (Musician, cook, decorator, writer, helper, teacher, leader, organizer, etc.)*

- *Whom do you have a heart for? What group of people are you drawn to work with? Is there an age group or special demographic? (Elderly, widows, those who are sick, single moms, teens, children, inner city, the lost, the homeless, students, women, men, young couples, young moms, etc.)*

- *How do you want to minister to them? (Would you use speaking gifts or serving gifts or both? What do you want to accomplish? What is your goal?)*

✦ *After answering these questions, how would you answer question 7 now?*

✦ *Reflect on Ephesians 2:10. How does this verse relate to Paul's words to Timothy?*

✦ *Spend time in prayer expressing thanks for your salvation and your calling. Ask Him to guide you in how to best live out your purpose and be faithful. (You may want to write out your prayer.)*

"I've had to learn that when God calls, He doesn't muffle His voice. If you're willing to be useful in His hands, you can be confident that He won't waste the gifts He's already entrusted to you. Calling is not about accomplishments, status, and titles but remaining in relationship with the one we serve."[2]

—Maggie Wallem Rowe

DAY THREE

Be Faithful to Know Your Savior

When life becomes challenging and I start to get anxious about how something will play out, it helps to remember how God has worked in past situations. Reflecting on His faithfulness gives me peace that He will take care of me in whatever situation I face today or will encounter in the future. Knowing our Savior and His attributes gives us confidence to persevere even in the most difficult circumstances. The more we get to know Him, the more we'll trust Him each day. Paul knew his Savior well, and he modeled to Timothy and others how to trust God. How well do we know our Savior?

Before falling asleep at night, I often go through the alphabet and focus on His attributes that start with each letter. Reflecting on His character deepens my love for Him and confidence in Him, no matter what is happening around me. As we ponder just one verse today, ask God to draw you into a deeper intimacy with Him.

Father, I love You. Thank You for all You've done for me. But most of all, thank You for who You are. You are all-powerful. You are faithful. You are sovereign. You are loving. You will never leave me. The more I know You, the more I love and trust You. Keep me faithful.

Looking to God's Word

2 Timothy 1:12

1. *Paul begins this verse with the phrase, "For this reason." To what is he referring?*

2. *What stands out to you from this verse?*

3. *Describe Paul's attitude in his suffering as a prisoner for the gospel. Why was he willing to suffer for the gospel? (Look for clues in the context.)*

4. *How would knowing "whom I have believed" help Paul (and us) not be ashamed of the gospel and suffer well for it?*

5. *Paul said in verse 12, "I am convinced that He is able to protect what I have entrusted to Him until that day." Commentators are divided on what it is that Paul has entrusted to Him. Some think he's referring to his salvation. Others see it as the gospel. Another view is Paul's life and his ministry. Do you have another idea? What do you think Paul is referring to and why?*

6. *What and when is "that day" Paul refers to in this verse? Read 1 Corinthians 1:7–8 and 2 Timothy 4:8. What insight do these passages give?*

Looking Upward

7. *How do you view God in the middle of suffering? What questions come to mind?*

8. What helps you walk through times of suffering and hardship?

Looking Deeper

9. As we close this day's study, let's read the words of another apostle—Peter. How did Peter encourage his readers in their suffering? What encourages you from each of these verses?

1 Peter 4:19

1 Peter 5:6–11

Looking Reflectively

We may not be suffering for our faith today, but we may suffer in other ways—a disease that takes away our vitality, an unfair situation at work, betrayal by a close friend, a wayward child, the loss of someone or something dear to us, or financial hardship. God knows what we're going through, and He walks alongside us through every trial.

During difficult seasons in my life, I didn't enjoy being there at the time, but now I can see how God was at work in me, drawing me into a deeper intimacy with Him as I was desperately dependent on His strength. God is always faithful, even when we question what He's doing and why He's doing it. He has a purpose. Will we remain faithful to Him?

✦ ***Are you suffering today? Are you in a difficult season of life? Write down what you know to be true about God and thank Him that He knows what He's doing and why. Surrender your life into His hands, trusting His sovereign plan for you.***

✦ ***Which Bible verses comfort and strengthen you in times of hardship?***

"Paul was persuaded that his entire case was in the best of hands. Even as he faced death, he had no misgivings. Jesus Christ was his Almighty Lord, and with Him there could be no defeat or failure. There was nothing to worry about. Paul's salvation was sure, and so was the ultimate success of his service for Christ here on earth."[3]

—William MacDonald

DAY FOUR

Be Faithful to Sound Doctrine

The internet gives us easy access to various doctrines floating around. Many are not sound. So, how do we remain faithful to God's Word and not be drawn away into false beliefs and teachings?

Timothy was dealing with false teachers in Ephesus who misused the Word of God for their own interests. Paul encouraged Timothy to stay faithful to the sound doctrine he had been taught. He understood the importance of the Word of God in transforming lives.

False teachers promote lies contrary to the Bible or taken out of context. As our world moves away from the truths of God's Word, will we remain steadfast and faithful, or will we get caught up in the world's way of thinking? Let's be examples of those who remain faithful to the Word of God, even as false doctrines and teachings bombard us. Stand firm!

Father, the world would love to pull us away from You and the truth of Your Word. Hold me close and keep me faithful. Keep me on guard against false doctrines and those who disregard Your Word. I need You, Lord.

Looking to God's Word

2 Timothy 1:13–14

1. *List Paul's two instructions to Timothy in verses 13–14.*

2. *What does he mean by "sound words" (v. 13)?*

3. *What would help us hold on to the example of sound words? What would hinder us?*

4. *What is the treasure Paul is referring to in verse 14? What insight does the New Living Translation (NLT) give? "Through the power of the Holy Spirit who lives within us, carefully guard the precious truth that has been entrusted to you."*

5. What does it mean to protect or guard through the Holy Spirit the treasure that has been entrusted to you (v. 14)?

Looking Upward

6. How would you recognize if someone is not teaching sound doctrine? What are some warning signs?

7. What are examples of false doctrines being taught today?

Looking Deeper

8. What results from unsound teaching according to 1 Timothy 1:3–7?

Looking Reflectively

Recently, I came across a short video of someone who considers himself a teacher of God's Word. Yet, as I listened, his message disturbed me. I found myself asking, *Where is that in the Bible? How did you come up with that interpretation of this verse?* Within a few minutes, I realized this wasn't the truth of God's Word, but the person was twisting the Scripture to say what he wanted it to say. The audience wanted their ears tickled, and that's precisely what he was doing. This was a timely reminder to be on guard against false teaching. It's all around us.

Don't become enamored with the lies of this world. Stay faithful to the truths of God's Word.

✦ *Ask God to search your heart and show you if you're in danger of listening to unsound doctrine and teaching. How can you protect against false doctrine?*

✦ *Spend some time in Psalm 19:7–11 and consider all God's Word has to offer. How does it change our lives?*

> *"Like Timothy, we need to pursue sound teaching and avoid all teaching that does not conform to the Scriptures, no matter how good certain teachers might sound or how large their following might be."*[4]
>
> —Earl D. Radmacher et al.

DAY FIVE

Be Faithful to Others

Faithful friends are a gift, and I'm grateful for those God has placed in my life who have stood by me through both the good times and the hard days. I will never forget the night I had to rush my elderly mom to the ER, not once, but twice, in the middle of the night. The second time, I felt helpless and distressed. I asked a couple in my church to meet me at the hospital if they could. They were waiting for us when we drove up, and they stayed with me until I had peace in the situation. They were faithful friends that night (and still are), even though it required sacrifice on their part. I long to be a faithful friend to others like they are to me.

Today, we'll examine a few relationships in Paul's life. One provides a positive example of faithfulness, while others paint a negative picture. Ask yourself: When people look at you, do they see a life that demonstrates faithfulness?

Lord, I desire to live a life of faithfulness, but sometimes, I fail.
Selfishness can kick in, or the world drowns out what I know is true and right.
Keep me faithful to You, Your Word, and others.

Looking to God's Word

2 Timothy 1:15–18

1. *What disappointment did Paul face in v. 15? To what do you think he was referring?*

2. *Contrast Phygelus and Hermogenes to Onesiphorus.*

3. *How did Onesiphorus demonstrate his faithfulness to Paul?*

4 *What did Paul ask the Lord to grant to Onesiphorus in verses 16 and 18?*

5. Why do you think he prayed in this way?

6. What is "that day" Paul refers to in verse 18? (You may want to refer to your answer to question 6 on Day 3.)

Looking Upward

7. Onesiphorus often refreshed Paul. What makes someone refreshing to be around? How do others refresh you?

Looking Deeper

8. Read John 15:13. How did Jesus demonstrate faithfulness in light of that verse? What would that look like for us?

Looking Reflectively

When we moved my mom from Louisiana to an assisted living here in Memphis, it felt overwhelming. There was so much that needed to be done, and my brother and I questioned if we would be able to take care of everything by ourselves. However, when we drove up to her new home to move her in that Saturday morning, a group from my church was waiting for us, ready to lend a hand in any way they could. We were blown away as they helped us unload furniture and boxes, set up the apartment, decorate, and even return the U-Haul. They refreshed us by coming alongside us in a time of need, and we're forever grateful for their generosity and support.

Onesiphorus refreshed Paul. We don't know specifically what he did, but we do know his actions had a positive effect. Perhaps he refreshed Paul through his words, or sitting beside him in silence, just being there for him, giving him a hug, or serving him in a tangible way. This should prompt us to ask ourselves, *Am I refreshing to others? Am I a faithful friend?*

✦ *Would others describe you as a Phygelus/Hermogenes (a fair-weather friend) or an Onesiphorus (a refresher)? What can you do to refresh someone today?*

✦ *What are some things that could hinder you from being faithful to others? How can you grow in this area?*

✦ *Ponder the words of 1 Samuel 12:24 from the New Living Translation (NLT): "But be sure to fear the Lord and faithfully serve him. Think of all the wonderful things he has done for you." Make this your prayer today.*

This first chapter of 2 Timothy motivates us to live out our God-given calling every day, using the gifts He's entrusted to us until the day He takes us home. Let's be faithful to carry out His calling.

"We are on a journey toward the heavenly Jerusalem. God has put into our hands precious treasures—the gospel of Christ, the gifts and calling He has given us, the lives of those we are called to serve; we have been charged to watch and steward them carefully."[5]

—Nancy DeMoss Wolgemuth

WEEK THREE

Strength

Do you ever grow weary in the season God has you in? It may be parenting young kids, leading a ministry, working an all-consuming job, juggling multiple responsibilities, or caregiving for a loved one. There have been times I've felt worn out and discouraged, questioning if I could keep going. But God knows what we're feeling and what we need. As we cry out to Him, He will strengthen us through His Holy Spirit.

In this week's passage, Paul exhorts Timothy to stay strong in the faith—an exhortation we all need to follow. Life can become challenging, but let's not allow trials and obstacles to hinder us from doing what God has called and equipped us to do.

Paul reminded Timothy that we find strength, not in ourselves, but in the grace of the Lord. As we strive to live a life that matters, may our strength in God be evident to all around us, especially in difficult circumstances. Do others see God's strength in you? How can you point people to Jesus for strength in times of need? Let's look to His Word.

Memory Verse: 2 Timothy 2:1. Write it below.

DAY ONE

Overview

"Lord, I can't do this." Have you ever said those words? I did just this week when I was facing a daunting task that seemed impossible. But as I spent time in God's Word, He reminded me, "You're right, Crickett. You can't do this in your own strength, but I am sufficient for whatever I've called you to do. Draw from My strength."

Paul was a great encourager and exhorter. Timothy felt inadequate and weak at times, but Paul urged him to keep moving forward in the Lord's strength. May we encourage others in the same way. We begin this week's lesson by reviewing the entire passage. Ask God to speak through His Word in a fresh way today.

Father, I confess I'm feeling weak. I need You.
Thank You for strengthening me and knowing exactly what I need.
You never intended for me to walk this life in my own power.
Help me walk in Your strength.

Looking to God's Word

2 Timothy 2:1–13

1. *What are the commands in this passage? What does Paul exhort Timothy to do?*

2. *What is Paul's main emphasis?*

3. *Is there anything new that you noticed for the first time?*

Looking Upward

4. *What do you learn about God/Jesus from this passage?*

5. *How would Paul's words help you "be strong in the grace that is in Christ Jesus" (v. 1)?*

Looking Deeper

6. *Read Ephesians 6:10–12. How does Paul's exhortation give further insight into being strong in the Lord?*

Looking Reflectively

Several friends of mine have recently been diagnosed with cancer. Instead of crumbling under the disappointing news and shaking a fist at God or questioning His love, they have demonstrated strength and peace in God. Yes, they've had moments of tears, discouragement, and heartache. But they've been surrounded by friends in prayer, and they are able to entrust their lives into God's faithful, loving hands, knowing He has a purpose in everything. What an encouragement to those of us around them. It is evident that their strength lies not in themselves, a doctor, or a treatment, but in the Lord and His sovereignty.

Is there something going on in your life today that's causing you to feel weak and needy? Don't be discouraged. Turn to the Lord and find strength in Him. He is aware of every situation you face, and He knows how to lead you forward in His strength.

✦ *In what areas are you feeling weak today?*

✦ *What schemes is the enemy Satan using against you?*

✦ *Pray through Isaiah 40:29–31. You may want to write these verses below in your own words.*

"When difficulty exposes the weakness of your resolve and the limits of your strength, you do not have to panic, because he will endure even in those moments when you don't feel able to do so yourself."[1]

—Paul David Tripp

DAY TWO

Be Strong in Teaching Others

We often think that teaching only happens in a classroom. However, teaching also occurs in various informal settings—around a table for a meal or coffee, in the car, or while walking with someone. It may look like sharing about a personal situation or imparting wisdom for dealing with a conflict or decision. Sometimes, those informal teaching situations are the most powerful.

I am grateful for those who have helped deepen my faith through their teaching—both formally and informally. They encouraged me when I felt weak or inadequate and reminded me where my strength is found. And I've been able to pass on to others what I learned from them.

Paul lived a life that mattered. He exhorted and encouraged Timothy to make a difference by teaching others what he was learning. I pray we will do the same.

How have people encouraged you to be strong in the Lord? Are you passing along to those around you what you've been learning? Ask God to teach you from His Word today.

Father, thank You for bringing people into my life who have spurred me on in my faith—people who have loved me, prayed for me, and spoken the truth in love. Help me do the same with others. Make me sensitive to the needs of those around me.

Looking to God's Word

2 Timothy 2:1–2

1. *Paul begins with another "therefore." How is verse 1 related to the previous verses (1:15–17)?*

2. *What does it mean to "be strong in the grace that is in Christ Jesus"? How do we do that?*

3. *What does it mean to entrust something to someone?*

4. *Why is it important to entrust what you've learned to faithful men/ women? Why do you think he emphasizes* faithful*?*

Looking Upward

5. How would you characterize a faithful person in this context? What qualities would you look for?

6. What might hinder us from passing along to others what we've been taught? How can we remedy that?

Looking Deeper

7. Read 1 Thessalonians 2:1–6. What do you learn about Paul's teaching and the motivation behind it?

Looking Reflectively

When I was on staff with Cru (formerly Campus Crusade for Christ), they emphasized spiritual multiplication: leading someone to Christ, discipling them so they could take what they've learned and pass it on to someone else, who would then pass it on to another, and so forth. To do that, we would have to make our teaching transferable—easy to teach and easy to remember. I still share some of the lessons my disciplers taught me in college and my early years on staff with Cru.

You can probably remember teachings shared by a pastor, teacher, or friend that hit home and have stayed with you throughout the years. Have you passed those lessons along to others or kept them for yourself?

✦ *Who is someone you can share what you're learning with? What do you want to entrust to them? What are some signs you might be drawing from your own strength rather than the Lord's?*

✦ *Write out Psalm 71:17–19. Spend time in prayer, asking God to make you sensitive to the needs of those around you and to guide you in initiating conversations. Be willing and available. Draw from God's strength, not your own.*

*"God has deposited with His people the truth of the Word of God.
It is our responsibility to guard this treasure and pass it on to others.
The task of the local church is not to preserve the truth, as in a museum;
but to live it and to teach it to the generations to come."*[2]

—Warren Wiersbe

DAY THREE

Be Strong Like a Soldier

Timothy was struggling, so Paul exhorted him to be strong in the grace that is in Christ Jesus. When you hear the word *strength*, what do you visualize? Perhaps you see a picture of a massive tree with deep roots, standing firm against destructive winds. Or maybe you think of an action figure or a person with big muscles (and maybe a cape). It may be a person you know who never breaks, regardless of what they're facing.

To help Timothy understand what strength in the Lord looks like, Paul provided three examples: a soldier, an athlete, and a farmer. All three face challenges in their respective responsibilities. We can learn much from them and how they continue to move forward. Today, we'll focus on the soldier.

Father, I want to be a good soldier, faithful to serve and honor You. Help me keep my focus on You and not let distractions of the world weaken that commitment. I love You, Lord.

Looking to God's Word

2 Timothy 2:3–4

1. *Write these two verses below, underlining any words or phrases that stand out.*

2. *Suffering hardship is a recurring theme for Paul in this letter (2 Tim. 1:8; 2:3, 9; 4:5). Why do you think Paul kept emphasizing suffering and hardship to Timothy?*

3. *What qualities make a good soldier? How does Paul describe a soldier in verse 4?*

4. *What is the goal of a good soldier? What's his purpose?*

5. What does Paul mean by the affairs of everyday life? What are some examples? How do they entangle us?

Looking Upward

6. Why is it essential that we not get tied up in the affairs of everyday life?

7. How do we avoid getting entangled?

Looking Deeper

8. What do you learn about suffering and hardship from the passages below? How should you respond, and why? How does God use them for good?

James 1:2–4

2 Corinthians 12:7–10

Looking Reflectively

My dad was a soldier in World War II. Even though that was before I was born, I later heard stories of his time in Germany and what it was like to fight as a soldier. You couldn't let your guard down, and there were times you were scared. You were part of a team; you knew your purpose; and you did everything you could to carry out that purpose. I've never been a soldier in that sense, fighting in a physical war. But I do have a role as a soldier for Jesus Christ. All believers do.

Every day, we fight a spiritual battle. The enemy doesn't want us to fight hard, stay focused, remain united, or stand firm. Satan wants us to give in and give up. Our goal is to remain strong in Christ's strength and serve Him faithfully as His soldier.

✦ *What does it mean to you to be a soldier for Jesus? What does that look like? Consider Paul's description in verse 4.*

✦ *A good soldier wants to please the one who enlisted him (v. 4). What commands in the New Testament come to mind that would please the Lord as we obey? (For instance, Philippians 2 gives us several.)*

Are there commands you know you're not obeying?

✦ *Reflect on Hebrews 12:1–3 in light of today's Scripture. How does this passage spur you on to be a good soldier for Christ?*

"As the soldier must leave all other pursuits, so the disciple must place his or her self at complete disposal to the kingdom of God."[3]

— Gary Demarest and Lloyd Ogilvie

DAY FOUR

Be Strong Like an Athlete and Farmer

Yesterday, we studied the example of a good soldier who follows and serves Christ. Today, we'll look at two additional examples Paul used—the athlete and the farmer. I tried athletics in high school, but I wasn't good at any sports. However, I've seen the discipline it takes to be a good athlete, and I have the utmost respect for them.

I've also never had experience as a farmer, although my grandfather owned a large farm. When I spent time with my grandparents in the summers, Grandpa would take me with him as he went about the day's chores, often before the sun came up. I saw firsthand how hard farmers work and the discipline it takes to produce healthy crops and care for animals.

Be attentive to what God wants to teach you from these examples of the soldier, athlete, and farmer. How do they exemplify strength?

Father, You desire for us to grow strong and produce fruit as Your children.
Help me keep my focus on You and carry out Your purpose.
Protect me from becoming undisciplined in my relationship with You.
Thank You for giving me all I need to follow and serve You wholeheartedly.

Looking to God's Word

2 Timothy 2:5–7

1. *Paul begins this section with the example of an athlete. What is the goal of an athlete? What's required for him to accomplish that goal?*

2. *What is the goal of a farmer? What's required for him to accomplish that goal?*

3. *What do these three examples (soldier, athlete, farmer) have in common?*

4. *What do you think Paul was trying to convey in verse 7?*

Looking Upward

5. *The athlete must compete according to the rules to win. What rules do we need to follow in life to run the Christian race and finish well?*

6. *How can you apply the lessons from these three examples (soldier, athlete, and farmer) to your own life today?*

Looking Deeper

7. *What lessons can you learn from 1 Corinthians 9:24–27 as they relate to Paul's message to Timothy in 2 Timothy 2? What stands out to you from this passage?*

   1 Corinthians 9:24–27

   "Do you not know that those who run in a race all run, but only one receives the prize? Run in such a way that you may win. Everyone who competes in the games exercises self-control in all things. So they do it to obtain a perishable wreath, but we an imperishable. Therefore I run in such a way as not to run aimlessly; I box in such a way, as to avoid hitting air; but I strictly discipline my body and make it my slave, so that, after I have preached to others, I myself will not be disqualified."

Looking Reflectively

Recently, I had the honor of sharing at the memorial service for a dear friend and mentor. As I reflected on her life, the first thing that came to mind was that she lived a life that mattered. She had made a difference for eternity as she poured into the lives of younger women, training and encouraging them to become more like Christ. She left a legacy that will continue for many years to come.

We can all think of people who have lived their lives well and for the glory of God—people who made a difference of eternal significance. But just like a soldier, farmer, and athlete, they faced challenges. God never promised the Christian life would be easy. It takes discipline, focus, obedience, and hard work to finish well, but the end result will be worth it. Will we finish well for the Lord?

✦ *In which of these areas (discipline, focus, obedience, hard work) are you strong?*

✦ *In which of these areas do you need to grow and strengthen in order to finish well? What are some specific things you can do?*

"Like soldiers, we have to give up worldly security and endure rigorous discipline.
Like athletes, we must train hard and follow the rules.
Like farmers, we must work extremely hard and be patient.
But we keep going despite suffering because of the thought of victory,
the vision of winning, and the hope of harvest."[4]

—Bruce Barton et al.

DAY FIVE

Be Strong Like Jesus

We all find ourselves at some point in overwhelming situations when we question how or if we'll be able to get through another day. God's Word reminds us that His strength will carry us through, not our own efforts. I've seen that to be true as God has brought me through tough circumstances that stretched me beyond my limitations. He has never let me down.

Paul began this week's passage by exhorting Timothy to "be strong in the grace that is in Christ Jesus" (2:1). Our strength is found in Him. Jesus demonstrated through His life how to stand strong, regardless of what is happening to us—physical pain, rejection, opposition, betrayal, or disappointment. In today's passage, Paul focuses on Jesus Christ. He set the example for how to live the Christian life. Ask God to make you more like Christ every day.

Jesus, I want to be more like You.
Help me walk in Your strength and power,
not my own. Teach me from Your life.
I pray that others see You in me.

Looking to God's Word

2 Timothy 2:8–13

1. *Why would Paul exhort Timothy to remember Jesus Christ in this context? How would that be beneficial to Timothy?*

2. *What does Paul point out about Jesus to Timothy in this passage?*

3. *Why was Paul willing to suffer hardship and endure all things? How would you describe his attitude?*

4. *What do you think Paul meant when he said, "the word of God is not imprisoned" (v. 9)?*

5. List the truths Paul lays out in verses 11–13. Why do you think Paul emphasized these truths to Timothy?

6. What does it mean in verse 13, "If we are faithless, He remains faithful, for He cannot deny Himself"?

Looking Upward

7. How does it encourage you to know that God is faithful even when we are faithless? How have you seen this to be true in your life?

Looking Deeper

8. Read Philippians 1:12–20. Paul had a great attitude toward others. What do you learn from Paul's attitude and his circumstances from these verses?

Looking Reflectively

We don't know what God has ahead for us. He leads us step by step and doesn't give us the entire blueprint all at once. This requires trusting Him and walking by faith corner to corner. When we face trials and difficulties, will we trust Him? Will we draw our strength from Jesus or try to navigate the challenges on our own? Let's cling to Him and allow Him to work in our lives, preparing us for whatever lies ahead.

Are you living a life characterized by God's strength? Are you demonstrating to the generations behind you how to live in a way that honors God in the face of hardship? Are you helping them find their strength in the Lord?

✦ *Whom have you seen demonstrate strength in Christ in the face of hardship and trials? How did they stand strong? What did you learn from them?*

✦ *How are you reflecting strength in Christ today?*

✦ ***Read Psalm 59:16–17. How does David express his strength in God? Use David's words to guide you through a time of prayer.***

"Lord, I feel like such a weakling most of the time—exhausted long before the day or the duties give out. Thank You for constant reminders that You are my strength, even (perhaps especially) when I feel I have none at all. Help me do the impossible, through You. Amen."

—Lucinda Secrest McDowell

WEEK FOUR

Diligence

We typically associate the word *diligent* with someone who is a hard worker—dedicated to completing a task, focused on what they're doing, and zealous to accomplish what they've set out to do. But we don't often think of diligence in relation to the words we speak. Paul reminds Timothy that we should be diligent in how we use our words, especially in teaching the Word of God. What we say can lead others astray from the truth of God's Word if we're not careful to protect and preserve it.

In this next section of Paul's second letter to Timothy (2:14–26), he focuses on the importance of how we use our words when teaching the Bible. Some in the church were teaching false doctrine, so Paul challenged Timothy to be diligent in speaking the Word of God wisely and guarding against those who would attempt to lead them astray from the true gospel with their words.

What do your words reveal about your love for the Lord and His Word? What do they reveal about your commitment to unity in the body of Christ and loving others? Are you speaking sound doctrine? Let's be diligent to handle the truth of God accurately (v. 15).

Memory verse: 2 Timothy 2:15. Write it below.

DAY ONE

Be Diligent to Guard Your Words

Have you ever said something, and then immediately wished you could take back your words and erase them? It may have been in a moment of anger or pain, or maybe you used God's Word out of context. The truth is, we can't erase our words once they're spoken.

This week, we'll focus on 2 Timothy 2:14–26. Read the entire passage today to get an overview of its content. In these verses, Paul exhorts Timothy to be diligent in "accurately handling the word of truth" (2:15). Do we teach the truth of God's Word, or do we stretch it to say what we want it to say? Not only are we to be diligent in guarding the words we speak, but we must also be careful as we listen to what others are teaching. If we're not, we can easily be lured into heresy.

Before continuing, ask God to help you be diligent in guarding your words.

Father, there's a lot of false teaching around us, even from some who consider themselves Christians. Protect me from falling prey to heresy and keep me from speaking words that are not Your truth. Keep me diligent to honor You in all I say and do. Guard my heart and mind, Lord.

Looking to God's Word

2 Timothy 2:14–26

1. *What does Paul command Timothy to do in this passage? What does he emphasize?*

2. *Today, we'll focus on the first imperative in verse 14. Who is the "them" to whom Paul is referring?*

3. *What are "these things" that Timothy is to remind them of? Why would they be important?*

4. *What does it mean to dispute about words in verse 14?*

5. *Why would that be useless and lead to the ruin of the listeners (v. 14)?*

Looking Upward

6. What issues do we dispute in the church today that we shouldn't be arguing over?

7. Some things, like the non-negotiables of the faith, are worth standing up for and defending. What are some non-negotiables of our Christian faith?

Looking Deeper

8. What additional insight does Paul give in 1 Timothy 6:3–5?

Looking Reflectively

One area we sometimes disagree on as believers is how the end times will unfold. I have an opinion, but I choose not to get drawn into a heated discussion about it. What we **can** agree on is that Christ will return one day. We should focus on that promise and not get caught up in debating the details of how and when it will happen. Regardless of the timing and specifics of the end times, I will live my life the same—living each day as if He could return at any moment and sharing Christ with those around me while there's still time.

Defend the essentials of the faith, but let's not allow the enemy to pull us into meaningless and fruitless debates. Be diligent in using your words wisely.

✦ *Is there something you're debating with others that isn't worth arguing about? Perhaps it's a preference or an opinion of how something should be done in the church. Ask God to search your heart and show you if there are things you're arguing about that He wants you to release.*

✦ *Make Colossians 4:5–6 your prayer. Write it in your own words.*

"Fighting about words carries the implication of splitting hairs or fighting about minor things that make no real difference. Splitting theological hairs and turning disagreements about minor matters into major battles is in no way profitable. It does not benefit the individuals, or the church."[1]

—Michael Martin

DAY TWO

Be Diligent to Handle God's Word Accurately

One of my biggest fears as a Bible teacher is that I will teach something incorrectly. That's why it takes me so long to prepare a talk on a passage—I want to ensure I teach Scripture accurately. As Christians, whether we're teaching in an official role or just sharing the Word with someone over coffee, we need to be careful in how we use the Word of God. It's easy to take verses out of context and make them say what we want or interpret them in ways never intended by the original author. Paul reminded Timothy of the importance of accuracy and integrity when teaching—or even discussing—Scripture. It's a good reminder for us today. Ask God to show you if you're misinterpreting His Word in any way.

Father, I pray for diligence to handle Your Word accurately.
Keep me sensitive to the Holy Spirit's prompting when
I'm getting away from the truth of Your Word.
Give me Your insight as I study and teach.

Looking to God's Word

2 Timothy 2:14–18

1. *What is Paul's command or imperative to Timothy in verse 15?*

2. *What does it mean to "present yourself approved to God as a worker who does not need to be ashamed" in verse 15? How do we do that?*

3. *What does Paul exhort Timothy to avoid and why (vv. 16–17)?*

4. *What do we learn about Hymenaeus and Philetus in verses 17–18?*

Looking Upward

5. *Paul exhorts Timothy to "avoid worldly and empty chatter" (v. 16). He's not talking about gossip or slander here. What do you think he's referring to in light of verse 18?*

6. How can that type of speech lead to further ungodliness?

Looking Deeper

7. Circle any examples of worldly and empty chatter mentioned in the following passages. How do these examples compare to your answer in Question 5?

1 Corinthians 15:12

"Now if Christ is preached, that He has been raised from the dead, how do some among you say that there is no resurrection of the dead?"

1 Timothy 1:3–4

"Just as I urged you upon my departure for Macedonia, to remain on at Ephesus so that you would instruct certain people not to teach strange doctrines, nor to pay attention to myths and endless genealogies, which give rise to useless speculation rather than advance the plan of God, which is by faith, so I urge you now."

1 Timothy 6:20

"Timothy, protect what has been entrusted to you, avoiding worldly, empty chatter and the opposing arguments of what is falsely called 'knowledge.'"

Titus 3:9

"But avoid foolish controversies and genealogies and strife and disputes about the Law, for they are useless and worthless."

2 Peter 2:1–3

"But false prophets also appeared among the people, just as there will also be false teachers among you, who will secretly introduce destructive heresies, even denying the Master who bought them, bringing swift destruction upon themselves. Many will follow their indecent behavior, and because of them the way of the truth will be maligned; and in their greed they will exploit you with false words; their judgment from long ago is not idle, and their destruction is not asleep."

Looking Reflectively

I've heard people interpret specific Bible verses to say what they want to hear. For instance, they read Psalm 37:4: "Delight yourself in the Lord; and He will give you the desires of your heart." They interpret that verse to say, "God will give me whatever I desire." However, they overlook the prerequisite at the beginning: "Delight yourself in the Lord." As we delight ourselves in Him, our desires will align with His.

Paul exhorted Timothy (and all believers) to handle the Scriptures accurately. Let's be diligent and not interpret it according to what we want to hear or take verses out of context.

✦ *What precautions can you take to ensure you're not misusing God's Word?*

✦ ***What are examples of words that would cause disunity, tear others down, make someone stumble, or discourage others in their faith?***

✦ ***Meditate on Psalm 119:33–35. Make this your prayer today, along with the memory verse this week.***

"One of our greatest needs as followers of Christ is to become people of the Word so that our prayers and our responses are saturated with God's way of thinking. Each of us should be able to use the Word effectively, not only in our worship and our own walk but also in ministering to others."[2]

—Nancy DeMoss Wolgemuth

DAY THREE

Be Diligent to Abstain from Wickedness

We live in a fallen world, and sin is all around us—hatred and division (even division among Christians), violent and senseless crime, flagrant disrespect for God and His Word, and rampant sexual sin. How are we responding?

How do the younger generations view us? Would they describe our lives as meaningful, a life that makes a difference and has eternal significance? Are we any different from the world? Do we shine God's light, living to please Him? Or are we enticed by the world's views and join in their actions, or condone them?

Paul exhorted Timothy to be diligent in abstaining from wickedness. If we're not diligent, why would the generations behind us be any different? Ask God to show you if there is an area you need to confess and turn away from.

Father, I feel the world's pull every day. Keep me standing firm in You. Protect me from giving in to the temptations around me. Help me live my life in a way that glorifies and points others to You.

Looking to God's Word

2 Timothy 2:19

1. *Today we'll focus on 2 Timothy 2:19. Write it below.*

2. *Paul talks about the firm foundation of God in this verse. What comes to mind when you hear the phrase firm foundation? What are the implications?*

3. *There are several views on what the firm foundation of God is: the church, God's truth, the gospel, and Jesus. However, most scholars agree that Paul is referring to the church (His people who stand strong in His truth). How do these passages support this view?*

   Ephesians 2:19–22

   1 Timothy 3:15

4. The firm foundation has a seal. One of my seminary professors, Dr. Tom Constable, explains in his commentary that "seals in New Testament times indicated ownership, security, and authenticity."[3] What are the two inscriptions on the seal (2 Tim. 2:19), and how do they affirm ownership, security, and authenticity?

Looking Upward

5. How does it encourage you today to know the firm foundation of God stands?

6. What are some practical steps we can take to guard against falling into sin?

Looking Deeper

7. What additional insight does John 10:27–28 give concerning the first inscription on the seal: "The Lord knows those who are His"?

8. How do the following verses affirm the second inscription on the seal: "Everyone who names the name of the Lord is to keep away from wickedness"?

1 Corinthians 6:19–20

"Or do you not know that your body is a temple of the Holy Spirit within you, whom you have from God, and that you are not your own? For you have been bought for a price: therefore glorify God in your body."

1 Peter 1:15–16

"But like the Holy One who called you, be holy yourselves also in all your behavior; because it is written: 'You shall be holy, for I am holy.'"

Looking Reflectively

Just as Timothy was dealing with false teachers in Ephesus, we have false teachers today who distort or deny the truth. Their words may vary and change through the years, but God's Word never changes. As we build into the younger generations, we must diligently follow God's truth and rely on the Holy Spirit to protect us from sin and false teaching. The firm foundation of God stands and will stand for eternity. As believers, our lives belong to Him. He has sealed us as His own with His Holy Spirit. As a result, we should live holy lives and not indulge in those things that displease and dishonor God.

✦ *Is there something you're doing that you would not want your children or others to do? If so, what needs to change? Ask God to help you make those changes.*

✦ *God's Word is our standard to live by. Are you listening to any teachings that are controversial and oppose God's Word?*

✦ *How can you encourage the next generations to stand firm in God's Word and keep away from sin?*

"The Lord knows those who are His because He can discern the heart, but all that the world can look at is the outward life. My friend, the world certainly makes sin look attractive by clever advertisements on billboards. How do we as believers compare? Are our lives an attractive advertisement for Christ?"[4]

—J. Vernon McGee

DAY FOUR

Be Diligent to Be an Implement for Honor

Paul encouraged Timothy to be diligent in using his words wisely, in handling God's Word accurately, and in abstaining from wickedness and sin. Today, we look at his exhortation to be an implement (vessel) that honors the Master, and what that would look like in our lives.

If you were coming to my home for dinner, I would never consider serving you with dirty forks, knives, and spoons that hadn't been cleaned for weeks. Why? Because I want to honor you by serving with cleanliness. In the same way, we should desire to honor and please God by serving Him with clean hearts, confessing our sins.

As you study the passage today, ask yourself, *Am I willing to be used by God and bring Him honor? Am I dishonoring Him in any way? Am I clean, or am I stained by the world? Ask God to work in you to make you an implement of honor.*

Father, I want to honor You with my words, my actions, and my life. Convict me of my sin so I can confess and be a cleansed vessel, ready to be used by You. Help me be diligent to honor and serve You every day.

Looking to God's Word

2 Timothy 2:20–21

1. *What do you think the large house in verse 20 represents in light of verse 19?*

2. *Whom do the honorable implements represent? Whom do the dishonorable implements represent?*

3. *How does someone become an implement for honor according to verse 21? What are "these things"?*

4. *How does Paul describe an implement for honor in verse 21?*

Looking Upward

5. *What determines if we are an honorable or dishonorable implement/ vessel?*

Looking Deeper

6. *How does God prepare us for every good work according to the verses below? What verses would you add?*

2 Corinthians 9:8

"And God is able to make all grace overflow to you, so that, always having all sufficiency in everything, you may have an abundance for every good deed."

Ephesians 2:10

"For we are His workmanship, created in Christ Jesus for good works, which God prepared beforehand so that we would walk in them."

2 Timothy 3:16–17

"All Scripture is inspired by God and beneficial for teaching, for rebuke, for correction, for training in righteousness; so that the man or woman of God may be fully capable, equipped for every good work."

Looking Reflectively

Years ago, a wise mentor told me, "Don't pray to be used by God. Pray that God will make you usable." I've never forgotten those words, and they have shaped my prayers over the years. To be used by God, we have to be willing for Him to make us usable, which may involve hardship and stretching our faith. Are we willing for Him to work in us as He chooses?

Let's not waste our lives focused on accumulating temporal things that won't last or building a name for ourselves, but let's invest in building His kingdom and honoring the Master with a clean heart.

✦ *Are you a vessel or implement of honor useful to the Master? If not, what areas are bringing dishonor to Him? Ask God to cleanse those areas.*

✦ *How have you seen God use you for His honor?*

"The choices you and I make each day either tarnish us or polish us to a higher degree of purity and usefulness."[5]

—Lawrence O. Richards

DAY FIVE

Be Diligent to Pursue Becoming Like Christ

How are you different in your relationship with Christ today than you were a year ago? Are you more like Christ now than this time last year? If not, why? We should strive to become more like Him every day and not settle for the status quo in our relationship with Him. Some questions to ponder this week:

- How are your actions reflecting Christ to the generations behind you?
- Do they see you arguing and debating things that, in light of eternity, are not important?
- Do they see you modeling the Christian life in such a way that it draws them to Christ?
- Does your life motivate others to desire to become more like Christ? Or do your actions turn them away from the Savior?
- How do you respond to those who disagree with your beliefs and values?

Today, we'll focus on Paul's exhortation to Timothy to pursue becoming more like Christ. Let's be diligent to do the same.

Jesus, I want to become more like You, but there are days
my actions and words don't reflect that. Forgive me for
those times I don't react to situations in a Christ-like manner.
Help me be attentive to the Holy Spirit's guidance.
Strengthen me in my weakness. I love You, Lord.

Looking to God's Word

2 Timothy 2:22–26

1. *What are Paul's commands and exhortations to Timothy? What does he want him to flee? What does he want him to pursue?*

2. *What are some examples of youthful lusts? How do we run from them?*

3. *How do we pursue righteousness, faith, love, and peace?*

4. *What is the significance of the phrase "with those who call on the Lord from a pure heart" in verse 22?*

5. List the qualities of the Lord's bond-servant in verses 24–26.

6. Why would these qualities be important as a bond-servant of the Lord (vv. 25–26)?

Looking Upward

7. Why do we sometimes find it hard to correct those who oppose God's truth and Christianity?

8. Why is gentleness important (v. 25)?

Looking Deeper

9. Read 1 Timothy 6:11–12. How does Paul's exhortation to Timothy relate to his exhortation in today's passage?

Looking Reflectively

How do we respond to those who disagree with the Bible? It's hard. We don't want to offend or argue, but there are times we need to speak up and defend the truth with gentleness. In some cases, their salvation may even be at stake. Jesus often used questions to dialogue with those who opposed His teachings. Share the gospel and explain why you believe the Word of God. Ask questions. Then leave the results in God's hands. Ask Him for wisdom in responding to those who disagree with His Word. As you become more like Christ, you will respond as He did to those who opposed His teachings.

✦ *As you look at the qualities of the Lord's bond-servant in verses 24–26, in which areas are you strong? Weak?*

✦ *What is one specific way you can apply this week's lesson to your life?*

"Here is wisdom: Fleeing is as important as pursuing. Our no is as important as our yes. And when we say no to unprofitable desires, we can then say yes to the best things. What should you flee? And what should you be running after?"[6]

—R. Kent Hughes and Bryan Chapell

WEEK FIVE

Vigilance

Recently, I was in the middle of a smash-and-grab in a store near my house shortly before noon. I was in the back, completely absorbed in looking at products I had come to purchase. Even though I heard glass shatter and a woman scream, I didn't even look up to see what was happening. I just assumed someone dropped some bottles and was upset. It wasn't until I started walking toward the checkout counter and saw the floor completely covered in glass that I realized a crime had occurred. But I was oblivious to what was going on because I wasn't vigilant; I wasn't on guard. Thankfully, the perpetrators didn't linger and rob each of us who were in the store. They were in a hurry to leave before the cops arrived. God reminded me that day to be vigilant—not just in my daily life, but also in my spiritual life.

In 2 Timothy 3:1–9, Paul gives Timothy a description of conditions that will exist in the last days, the time between Christ's first coming and His return. We are living in the last days now. Paul challenges Timothy and all believers to be alert and on guard during these times to avoid being drawn into the world's ways and compromising our values and beliefs. Let's be an example for the younger generations of how to be vigilant every day.

Memory Verse: 2 Timothy 3:1. Write it below.

DAY ONE

Be Vigilant in the Last Days

It saddens me to watch people moving away from the truths of God's Word. Sin has always existed, but it seems more magnified and glorified as we get closer to His return. Actions that clearly violate Scripture are considered acceptable by many. Christians are accused of being intolerant. But it's not a matter of being intolerant—it's a matter of being disturbed by the very things that break God's heart.

Paul vividly described the last days for Timothy, and he urged him to be on guard and remain vigilant. We'll begin this week's lesson by reviewing the passage as a whole and getting the big picture. Let's focus on what we can do to stay alert against our enemy Satan and live godly lives in an ungodly world.

Father, keep me vigilant about the things going on around me. Help me avoid complacency and apathy. Show me how to stand firm and shine the light of Christ in a dark world.

Looking to God's Word

2 Timothy 3:1–9

1. *As you read this passage, what is Paul's main emphasis? What words or themes are repeated?*

2. *Which characteristics mentioned by Paul in verses 2–5 focus on self?*

3. *Which characteristics have to do with relationships with others?*

4. *Which ones describe a perspective of living life without thinking of God?*

Looking Upward

5. *What disturbs you most about the times in which we live today? How are you responding?*

6. *How can you encourage your generation and train the generations behind you to live godly lives, regardless of the pressures and temptations they face? How can you help them stay vigilant?*

Looking Deeper

7. *What advice did Paul offer in his other letters concerning how to live in these times? List at least one principle from each verse or passage.*

Romans 13:11–14

"Do this, knowing the time, that it is already the hour for you to awaken from sleep; for now salvation is nearer to us than when we first believed. The night is almost gone, and the day is near. Therefore let's rid ourselves of the deeds of darkness and put on the armor of light. Let's behave properly as in the day, not in carousing and drunkenness, not in sexual promiscuity and debauchery, not in strife and jealousy. But put on the Lord Jesus Christ, and make no provision for the flesh in regard to its lusts."

Ephesians 5:11–13

"Do not participate in the useless deeds of darkness, but instead even expose them; for it is disgraceful even to speak of the things which are done by them in secret. But all things become visible when they are exposed by the light, for everything that becomes visible is light."

Colossians 4:2

"Devote yourselves to prayer, keeping alert in it with an attitude of thanksgiving."

Colossians 4:5

"Conduct yourselves with wisdom toward outsiders, making the most of the opportunity."

Looking Reflectively

Second Timothy 3:1–9 has few words of encouragement about the last days. Yet, we can still live victoriously in a corrupt world. Godly principles are often ridiculed and hated. Children are being indoctrinated with philosophies contrary to God's Word. Every day, we need to be vigilant and alert, not only to what is happening outside our doors but what is being piped directly into our homes via the wide-open window of the internet.

Just as in Paul's day, we need to be vigilant about what is happening around us today. It would be easy to be paralyzed by fear and discouragement, but we're not to stay hidden indoors and become depressed and anxious. Paul provides us with clear guidance on how to walk through such times. Be vigilant. Let's teach the next generations to be on guard, keeping our eyes fixed on Jesus.

✦ *Write out 1 Peter 5:8–9 and reflect on how to apply these verses daily.*

✦ *Spend some time in prayer. Be honest with God concerning your fears and concerns about the current culture/times. What is causing you to become anxious or fearful? How can you overcome that anxiety and fear?*

✦ *What is one practical thing you can do to stay vigilant?*

"But if 'difficult times' have been present off and on
for two millennia and beyond, then why do we wring our hands,
whining that surely this is the end of the world? God is still on the throne.
Whatever is happening in your world today . . .
it did not take Him by surprise."[1]

—Lucinda Secrest McDowell

DAY TWO

Be Vigilant Against Loving Self

I've heard it said many times, "This world is not our home." However, I must admit that I have enjoyed this world and all it offers . . . until recent years. Certain events or ways of life in our culture make me long for my eternal home where sin, pain, evil, and division don't exist.

Jesus could come back any day, and I'm ready for His return. But in the meantime, let's stay attentive, but also rest in God's sovereignty and power. Until Jesus returns, let's do our part to point people to Him.

Although Paul wrote these words in 2 Timothy 3 many years ago, they remain relevant to us now. Today we'll focus on the first few characteristics of people in the last days. Ask God to show you how to be vigilant as we navigate these challenging times.

*Father, help me love You more than anything or anyone else.
Keep me from setting my attention on things that will
never satisfy. Help me stand firm against the pull of the world.
Protect me from becoming discouraged and depressed in these times we live.
I need You, Lord.*

Looking to God's Word

2 Timothy 3:1–2

1. *In verse 1, Paul cautions Timothy that difficult times will come in the last days. The first characteristic he warns about is being a lover of self (v. 2). How would you recognize a lover of self?*

2. *The second characteristic Paul addresses is a lover of money (v. 2). What are the dangers of loving money?*

3. *The third characteristic is boastfulness. Is this the same as being a lover of self, or does it differ? If so, how?*

4. *The fourth characteristic is arrogance. How do you define arrogance? How does it manifest itself in someone's life?*

5. *What is the opposite of arrogance?*

6. *How do these characteristics negatively affect our relationship with God?*

Looking Upward

7. *What do these first four descriptions have in common? How do you see them lived out in our world today?*

8. *How can we be vigilant against these attitudes in our own lives?*

   —Loving self

   —Loving money

   —Boasting

   —Arrogance

Looking Deeper

9. *What insight do we gain from the following passages about these four areas?*

   Proverbs 14:16

   "A wise person is cautious and turns away from evil, but a fool is arrogant and careless."

Jeremiah 9:23–24

"This is what the Lord *says: 'Let no wise man boast of his wisdom, nor let the mighty man boast of his might, nor a rich man boast of his riches; but let the one who boasts boast of this, that he understands and knows Me, that I am the* Lord *who exercises mercy, justice, and righteousness on the earth; for I delight in these things,' declares the* Lord.*"*

Philippians 2:21

"For they all seek after their own interests, not those of Christ Jesus."

1 Timothy 6:9–10

"But those who want to get rich fall into temptation and a trap, and many foolish and harmful desires which plunge people into ruin and destruction. For the love of money is a root of all sorts of evil, and some by longing for it have wandered away from the faith and pierced themselves with many griefs."

Looking Reflectively

Our sin nature focuses on self, which we see demonstrated in various ways, including a lack of respect for God and others. But our focus should be on the One who created us, loves us, and provides for us. When we're inward focused, we can't see the needs of others. We put ourselves first.

During my first two and a half years in college, I put God in the back seat and told Him I would run my life my way. I was a lover of self, boastful, arrogant, and falsely believing I could run my life better than God could. It didn't take long for me to realize how wrong I was, and I stepped down from the throne of my life and surrendered to the Lord Jesus. I've never regretted that decision. He changed my life for His glory.

✦ *Ask God to search your heart and show you if any of these four characteristics are true in your life. If so, confess and ask Him to redirect your focus. Surrender to His Lordship.*

✦ *Write out and reflect on Philippians 2:3–4.*

"The question isn't, Will things get difficult? (They will.)
Nor, Is God in control? (He is.) The greater question is,
How do we live and minister in a world that has lost its way? . . .
What will it take to wake us so that we can impact a world
speeding faster than ever in the wrong direction?"[2]

—Charles Swindoll

DAY THREE

Be Vigilant Against Ungodly Attitudes

Are there certain things people do that make you angry or frustrated? One thing that irritates me is the sight of speeding cars weaving recklessly in and out of traffic or running red lights and yield signs, narrowly averting a horrible accident. There's no respect for others. I find myself screaming internally at the guilty one: *What is wrong with you?*

But I also need to examine my own heart and ask God to reveal *what's wrong with me*. What needs to change in my life—my attitudes, actions, and words? Today, we continue to examine the characteristics of people in the last days. Ask God to reveal if any of these are present in your life.

Father, keep me on my knees in prayer as we await Your return.
Show me how to respond to others and point them to You.
Reveal sin in my own heart. Keep me vigilant, Lord.

Looking to God's Word

2 Timothy 3:2–3

1. *Paul addresses slanderers in verse 2. What comes to mind when you hear the term* slanderers*?*

2. *The next characteristic is disobedience to parents. Why is disobedience to parents not pleasing to God? (See Ex. 20:12.)*

3. *Paul then addresses those who are ungrateful, unholy, unloving, and irreconcilable. Why would these characteristics be displeasing to God?*

4. *Paul continues by pointing out malicious gossip. What is the motivation behind malicious gossip? How does this relate to the first four descriptions found in verse 2?*

Looking Upward

5. How do you see these characteristics in our world today? Can you give a specific example?

6. How should we respond to those living in this way?

Looking Deeper

7. How do these verses below instruct us to live in contrast to 2 Timothy 3:2–3?

John 13:34

"I am giving you a new commandment, that you love one another; just as I have loved you, that you also love one another."

Romans 12:18

"If possible, so far as it depends on you, be at peace with all people."

2 Corinthians 7:1

"Therefore, having these promises, beloved, let's cleanse ourselves from all defilement of flesh and spirit, perfecting holiness in the fear of God."

Ephesians 4:29

"Let no unwholesome word come out of your mouth, but if there is any good word for edification according to the need of the moment, say that, so that it will give grace to those who hear."

1 Thessalonians 5:18

"In everything give thanks; for this is the will of God for you in Christ Jesus."

Looking Reflectively

My mom used to tell us, "If you don't have anything good to say about somebody, don't say anything at all." She lived that out in her own life and set an example for us as kids. I've often remembered her words when I'm about to open my mouth and engage in a negative or argumentative conversation that would not benefit anyone.

Our world has become more divided over the years, and we're growing weary of all the negative banter hurled toward one another. What could change if we used our words to encourage and build up instead of divide and tear down? We need to be vigilant about how we treat one another. Do we reflect Christ in our words and attitudes?

✦ *Review the characteristics in today's passage. Ask God to show you if any of these are true in your life. If so, what brought you to this place? What can you do to change?*

✦ *Make Psalm 139:23–24 your prayer today.*

✦ *How can you pray for others who are living in the way Paul describes?*

"Paul wants Timothy to know how bad these last days really are . . . To be forewarned is to be forearmed."[3]

—George W. Knight

DAY FOUR

Be Vigilant Against Ungodly Actions

I spent a summer in the Philippines while serving on staff with Cru, taking the *Jesus* film to hard-to-reach villages. We would spend the night camping out at each stop. Our team leaders always warned us to be vigilant if we needed to wander from the camp for any reason, especially at night. *Be watchful for snakes, spiders, and other critters that might attack you. Be cautious of hidden holes in the ground that could lead to broken ankles. Don't go anywhere alone.* We were to be watchful and alert for anything/anyone that could harm us and hinder the work God had called us to do.

In the same way, we are to be vigilant and watchful for those whom Paul describes in 2 Timothy 3. Today we'll continue to examine the characteristics of people in the last days. Many scholars believe Paul was describing the false teachers in Ephesus, as well as pointing out that these characteristics depict the nature of man in the last days, which will worsen as we get closer to His return. Let's learn from Paul's words to Timothy.

Father, keep me vigilant to all that's going on around me.
I want to shine Your light and point others to You.
Help me stay surrendered to You and available to be used as You desire.

Looking to God's Word

2 Timothy 3:3–5

1. *As you look at the next characteristics Paul points out, how would you define or describe each of these?*

   Without self-control

   Brutal

   Haters of good

   Treacherous

   Reckless

   Conceited

   Lovers of pleasure rather than lovers of God

2. *The final characteristic he mentions is "holding to a form of godliness, although they have denied its power" (v. 5). What do you think that means? How do we see that today?*

Looking Upward

3. *Paul instructs Timothy to "avoid such people as these" in verse 5. What did he mean? How do we do that and still reach out to those who need Christ?*

4. *In what ways can we be a light and point people to Jesus when the world increasingly disrespects God and His Word?*

Looking Deeper

5. *Read Galatians 5:19–21 where Paul describes the deeds of the flesh. How do these characteristics align with the ones Paul mentions in 2 Timothy 3:2–5?*

6. How does the fruit of the Spirit in Galatians 5:22–23 contrast with the deeds of the flesh?

Looking Reflectively

A friend shared with me about his sister who recently passed away. She had grown up in the church and a Christian home but began to drift when she moved away to college. Over the years, my friend had numerous conversations with his sister about Jesus and salvation through Him alone, but she couldn't accept that Jesus' death on the cross was enough to pay for her sins. She believed she had to work for her salvation.

One day, some people knocked on her door to talk with her about "God," and she invited them in. What they said supported her beliefs about works and drew her into a false gospel, introducing her to other gods and false doctrines. As they shared unbiblical ideas, their teachings began to draw in my friend's sister. She chose to believe the message of those who were "holding to a form of godliness, although they have denied its power" (2 Tim. 3:5). As a result, she wandered from the foundational truths of God's Word. When she passed away suddenly, my friend was devastated. "I don't know where my sister is spending eternity. But I pray that our conversations through the years about Jesus came back to her in her final hours on this earth."

False teachers have always been around and will be until Jesus returns. We must be vigilant at all times.

✦ *What are some influences in your life that might potentially have a negative effect on your spiritual life?*

✦ *What are some specific actions you can take to prevent the world from pulling you away from Christ and God's Word?*

✦ *Spend time in prayer, being honest with God about how you're feeling in these times. Write out Ephesians 5:15–16 below. Pray these verses back to God in your own words.*

"Only the gospel offers a radical solution to this problem. For only the gospel promises a new birth or new creation, which involves being turned inside out, from self to unself, a real reorientation of mind and conduct, and which makes us fundamentally God-centred instead of self-centred. Then, when God is first and self is last, we love the world God loves and seek to give and serve like him."[4]

—John Stott

DAY FIVE

Be Vigilant Toward the World

I once watched a documentary about a woman who was deceived by a man she met online. She thought he was looking for love, and he said all the right things to make her feel she could trust him, only to find out later he was merely interested in getting her money. Sadly, we read about numerous situations similar to that. There are deceivers all around us, looking for someone vulnerable and ready to be caught in their web of lies.

We must be vigilant against deception, not only in our physical desires, but also in our spiritual lives. As we discussed in Week 2 and see here again in 2 Timothy 3:5–9, there are false teachers ready to draw us away from the truth of God's Word by promising wonderful things from a false religion and presenting persuasive arguments. They prey on people's emotions and weaknesses and entice them to believe in a religion that only offers empty promises. How do we guard against that? Today we'll examine how the world tries to draw us away from the simplicity and devotion to Christ. Ask God to protect and keep you alert to those who would attempt to lead you astray.

Father, guard my heart and mind. Keep me vigilant to temptations of the world around me and the schemes of Satan. Give me an attentive heart to Your promptings. Guide me step by step. Thank You for walking this journey with me.

Looking to God's Word

2 Timothy 3:5b–9

1. *Describe the women who are captivated by those not following God (vv. 6–7).*

2. *Why would being weighed down with sins make us vulnerable to being led astray?*

3. *What are the "various impulses" that can lead us away from God (v. 6)?*

4. *How does Paul describe the people we're called to avoid (vv. 5–9)?*

5. What does it mean by "always learning and never able to come to the knowledge of the truth" in verse 7?

Paul gives an example in verse 9 of Jannes and Jambres, two men who opposed Moses. Peter Williams writes in his commentary: "Jannes and Jambres are not mentioned in Scripture, but according to Jewish tradition they were the magicians who opposed Moses with their counterfeit and magic. Warning Timothy, Paul refers to them as an illustration of those who distort God's Word."[5]

6. What does the phrase "men of depraved mind" mean in verse 8?

Looking Upward

7. What are subtle ways we see verse 6 happening in our culture today?

Looking Deeper

8. Read Jude 17–19. How did Jude describe people in the last time?

9. What wisdom does he give as to how to live in these days in Jude 20–23?

Looking Reflectively

Each day, I try to skim the news headlines to see what's happening in our country and world so I can pray specifically. But, at times, it just depresses me and causes me to ask God, *How are we ever going to see change? Lord, what can we do?*

It would be easy to lose heart, and we may wonder if there's any hope. Yes, there is. Our God is still on the throne and in control, no matter how crazy life may get.

One of my favorite birds is the male cardinal, looking so regal with his red robe and crown on his head. Every time I see this beautiful bird, it's a reminder to pause and praise God for His sovereignty.

How should we respond to troubling events unfolding today? Pray for God's mighty hand to work in the darkness and ask God to shine His light through us.

✦ *What is one thing in the world (church, government, or culture) that troubles you most? Where have you seen God working in spite of these issues?*

✦ *Write out Jude's benediction below from Jude 24–25. Spend time praying through these verses. Personalize them to your life and what you're dealing with today. Pray for His peace and strength to trust His loving hand even when you don't understand what He's doing.*

"Take hold of the Father's assurance,
and then say with strong courage, 'I will not fear.'
It does not matter what evil or wrong may be in our way,
because 'He Himself has said, "I will never leave you."'"[6]

—Oswald Chambers

WEEK SIX

Equipping

I was a cardiovascular perfusionist for eighteen years. (A perfusionist operates the heart-lung machine during open-heart surgery.) But before I could sit behind that machine and take someone's life into my hands, I had to be equipped. It took several years of training in the classroom and the operating room before I received my degree and was certified to carry out that responsibility. (And trust me, you wouldn't want someone who isn't equipped to run the heart-lung machine on you in surgery.)

It's also vital that we be equipped for the ministry God has called us to. I thank God for the women who discipled me through the organization Cru. They equipped me to study and teach God's Word, walk in the power of the Holy Spirit instead of my own strength, share Christ with others, and disciple women. As a result of their ministry to me, I knew I wanted to devote my life to discipling women and equipping them to do the same. What better way to leave a lasting legacy?

How has God equipped you to make a difference for the Lord? How are you equipping the younger generations with the Word of God to stand firm in their faith in an ever-changing world? Will they be prepared to face the challenges ahead?

Paul doesn't sugarcoat the Christian life. He's honest with Timothy and reminds him that following Christ will involve suffering and persecution, but it will be worth it. He was committed to equipping Timothy to stand firm when facing false teachers and persecution for his faith.

Memory Verse: 2 Timothy 3:16–17. Write it below.

DAY ONE

Equip by Example

July 1976 will always be etched in my memory. It was the first day of our annual summer staff training for Cru in Fort Collins, Colorado. As we gathered that Sunday morning, our leaders shared news that shook our world. Our Cru women leaders were on a retreat over the weekend in the Big Thompson Canyon and had to evacuate during the night because of a raging flood. Seven women didn't make it out and went home to be with the Lord. That week was powerful for all of us as we grieved the loss of these godly women. However, we were strengthened and encouraged by the testimonies of those who survived the flood as they shared with us some of their final moments with those we lost. They modeled by example how to face the unthinkable and move forward in the midst of tragedy. They wanted to equip us to handle whatever we would face in the future, and they accomplished that by their words and actions.

What kind of example are we setting for others? What kind of legacy are we leaving behind—a legacy of eternal significance or one that will have a negative impression or none at all? We can tell people what to do and how to do it, but words alone aren't sufficient. We need to demonstrate what we say by living it out.

Paul begins this section by affirming Timothy: *Timothy, in contrast to those who oppose the truth, you have followed* ***my example****.* Paul modeled a godly life for Timothy, and he wanted Timothy to do the same for those entrusted to him. In today's passage, we'll focus on the qualities in 2 Timothy 3:10–11.

Father, help me be a godly example to those around me.
Keep me from becoming complacent in living out Your truth.
Equip me to stand strong in tough times.

Looking to God's Word

2 Timothy 3:10–11

1. *In which areas did Timothy follow Paul's example?*

2. *In Paul's first letter to Timothy, what did Paul exhort him to do in 1 Timothy 4:12? How do these qualities relate to what he said in 2 Timothy 3:10?*

3. *Paul commended Timothy first for following his teaching (v. 10). What do we learn about Paul's teaching from 1 Timothy 4:6 and Acts 20:18–21?*

4. *In what ways was Timothy following Paul's conduct?*

5. He also commended Timothy for following his purpose. How did Paul state his purpose in Acts 20:24?

6. How did Paul demonstrate faith, patience, and love?

Looking Upward

7. What would motivate you to follow someone's example in these areas?

8. Which would be the hardest for you to model for others? Why?

Looking Deeper

9. Paul told the people of Corinth in 1 Corinthians 11:1, "Be imitators of me, just as I also am of Christ." If we are imitating Christ, what should our lives look like? What Scriptures would you look to for examples or commands for imitating Christ? (For instance, Col. 3:12–17.)

Looking Reflectively

There are numerous people I admire and want to be like because of their walk with God. Some model a powerful prayer life; others model trust in God regardless of their circumstances. Some share Christ everywhere they go and invest in discipling others. They are living lives that matter for eternity as they equip others to become more like Christ.

Paul equipped Timothy for the challenges he would face in this world. He modeled the Christian life, not only for Timothy but also for us today. Let's learn from Paul's example as we equip others.

✦ *What kind of example are you setting for the generations behind you? Pray through the questions below based on 2 Timothy 3:10–11 to guide you. Ask God to show you areas where you can grow, and ask Him to work in you, making you more like Him. You may want to journal your thoughts.*

Are you teaching and following sound doctrine? Or are you listening to or reading material that could lure you away from the true faith?

Are you conducting yourself in a God-honoring way that you want others to follow? Or is there an area that needs to change?

Do you know your purpose, and are you living it out, using your spiritual gifts and strengths for the Lord?

In what areas is your faith strong? Wavering?

Are you patient or impatient with others?

In what ways are you demonstrating love for others, even those hard to love?

Is there someone you're struggling to forgive?

Are you persevering in difficult times, putting your trust in God?

"Timothy had chosen to follow in the footsteps of Paul. He had seen the consistency of Paul's Christian commitment and sacrificial service. He had adopted the apostle as a role model as he served alongside him."[1]

—Luther Dorr

DAY TWO

Equip for Suffering

No one wants to suffer or go through persecution. Yet, the Bible makes it clear that suffering and hardship are part of the Christian life. I've experienced seasons when I "suffered" because of my faith. I've been made fun of, ostracized and left out of gatherings, told I was weak and needed a crutch (religion), faced rejection in relationships, and even "threatened" to be hung in effigy on the campus. You can probably share some examples from your own life. Suffering for Christ isn't just for missionaries and in countries that reject Christianity. It applies to all believers.

Becoming a Christian doesn't mean life will be full of rich blessings every day with no struggles. Jesus said we'd suffer for His sake (Phil. 1:29). He suffered and was persecuted. Paul suffered. As followers of Christ, we will also experience hard times. Those difficult seasons are the substance that deepens our faith. Are we equipped to stand firm when suffering comes? Are we equipping others to stay strong in their faith?

Father, I don't like to suffer, but I admit that it's during those times of hardship that I have grown the deepest in my intimacy with You.
Those difficult days have made me dependent on You as I admit my weakness.
Thank You for carrying me through those seasons.
Help me equip others to stand strong when the storms come.

Looking to God's Word

2 Timothy 3:10–11

1. *Today we'll look at the last three areas Paul mentioned to Timothy in these verses—perseverance, persecutions, and sufferings. Paul mentioned three cities where he encountered suffering: Antioch, Iconium, and Lystra. As you read what happened in each place, answer the following questions.*

   Acts 13:14, 42–52 (Antioch):

   a. Who persecuted them and why?

   b. How were they persecuted?

   c. What positive do you see in this situation?

   Acts 14:1–7 (Iconium):

   a. Who persecuted them and why?

b. How were they persecuted?

c. What positive do you see in this situation?

Acts 14:8–22 (Lystra):

a. Who persecuted them and why?

b. How were they persecuted?

c. What positive do you see in this situation?

2. *According to 2 Timothy 3:11, how did God respond to Paul's persecutions and sufferings?*

3. *What are some ways you've seen God respond in your life or in the lives of others?*

Looking Upward

4. *How are persecutions, suffering, and perseverance (endurance) related? How do they differ?*

5. *Can you think of a time when you had to endure hardship or suffering? How did you handle it? What helped you persevere?*

Looking Deeper

6. *I often turn to Isaiah 41:10 when I'm in the middle of a difficult time. As you read this verse, what does God tell us not to do, and what are His promises? How does He encourage us?*

Looking Reflectively

We face suffering in various forms and for different reasons. Sometimes we face difficulties because we disobey God, and He disciplines us. Other times, we face resistance, opposition, and rejection because we follow Christ. And sometimes we can't see why God has chosen for us to suffer. Even though we don't always understand why we're going through hardship, we can find peace in knowing that God works all things together in our lives for good and for His greater purpose.

He doesn't ask us to understand; He asks us to trust Him.

✦ *Are you experiencing suffering and hardship today? What are you facing? What positives can you see in this situation? How do you see God's hand at work? Pour out your heart to Him who cares for you (1 Peter. 5:7). Write down some verses that strengthen you during hardship.*

✦ *You may not be facing a hard time right now, but you probably know someone who is. Pray for them, asking God to strengthen and draw them closer to Him.*

"God never wastes pain. He always uses it to accomplish His purpose. And His purpose is for His glory and our good. Therefore, we can trust Him when our hearts are aching or our bodies are racked with pain. Trusting God in the midst of our pain and heartache means that we accept it from Him."[2]

—Jerry Bridges

DAY THREE

Equip to Suffer Well

One of my favorite autobiographies is *In the Arena* by Isobel Kuhn. As a missionary in China with the China Inland Mission in the 1940s, she endured much suffering as she followed God's leading. Yes, she would get discouraged, but she never gave up. Reading about her faith encourages me to be equipped and ready to handle suffering in the same way she did. She never lost hope because she kept her focus on her Savior, whom she loved deeply.

None of us wants to suffer, and when we do, we often ask, "Why me?" But nowhere in Scripture does God promise a life without pain and struggles. Jesus tells us in John 16:33 that we will have tribulation. The Bible gives us examples of godly men and women who suffered greatly. Joseph, Job, Naomi, and David all suffered in different ways. It's in those difficult seasons that we see the deepest growth in our relationship with God if we allow Him to work in us during those times. Today we'll focus on one verse that tells us what to expect as Christians who seek to live godly lives.

Lord, I want to follow You and become more like You,
but that requires seasons of struggle and hardship, including persecution.
Strengthen me during those times. Don't let me become bitter and
turn away from You. Hold me close when I face persecution for my faith.

Looking to God's Word

2 Timothy 3:12

1. *Write out this verse. What is Paul's message?*

2. *Why do you think this is true? Why is it necessary?*

3. *What forms of suffering and persecution did Paul go through in 2 Corinthians 11:23–27?*

4. *What was Paul's attitude toward suffering in Romans 8:18?*

5. *How does one develop that attitude?*

Looking Upward

6. *Why do you think God allows some believers to suffer or be persecuted for their faith more than others?*

Looking Deeper

7. *What additional insight about suffering and persecution do these passages give? What stands out to you from these verses?*

Matthew 5:10–12

"Blessed are those who have been persecuted for the sake of righteousness, for theirs is the kingdom of heaven. Blessed are you when people insult you and persecute you, and falsely say all kinds of evil against you because of Me. Rejoice and be glad, for your reward in heaven is great; for in this same way they persecuted the prophets who were before you."

John 15:18–21

"If the world hates you, you know that it has hated Me before it hated you. If you were of the world, the world would love you as its own; but because you are not of the world, but I chose you out of the world, because of this the world hates you. Remember the word that I said to you, 'A slave is not greater than his master.' If they persecuted Me, they will persecute you as well; if they followed My word,

they will follow yours also. But all these things they will do to you on account of My name, because they do not know the One who sent Me."

2 Corinthians 4:7–11

"But we have this treasure in earthen containers, so that the extraordinary greatness of the power will be of God and not from ourselves; we are afflicted in every way, but not crushed; perplexed, but not despairing; persecuted, but not abandoned; struck down, but not destroyed; always carrying around in the body the dying of Jesus, so that the life of Jesus may also be revealed in our body. For we who live are constantly being handed over to death because of Jesus, so that the life of Jesus may also be revealed in our mortal flesh."

Philippians 1:29–30

"For to you it has been granted for Christ's sake, not only to believe in Him, but also to suffer on His behalf, experiencing the same conflict which you saw in me, and now hear to be in me."

Looking Reflectively

Years ago, when I was facing a tough situation, a dear friend gently reminded me, "Crickett, God is more committed to building your character than preserving your comfort." As hard as those words were to hear, I've never forgotten them. She was right.

As I was writing this lesson, I had to confess I don't want to go through persecution and hardship. I prefer a life of comfort. However, I know that my deepest spiritual growth has occurred during the challenging days, not the easy ones. He has always given me the strength to get through those difficult seasons one day at a time. I don't enjoy the process, but I want the end result—becoming more like Christ.

God takes each of us on a different journey to develop perseverance and Christlikeness. He doesn't favor one person over another, but He has the same goal for all of us—to become completely sanctified, becoming more like Christ every day. And He takes us down different paths to get us there. One day we'll understand why.

✦ ***Spend time reflecting on Psalm 31:14–20.***

✦ ***Pray for Christians around the world who are being persecuted for their faith.***

"When you become weak through the fierce fires of affliction, do not try to 'be strong.' Just 'be still, and know that [He is] God.' And know that He will sustain you and bring you through the fire. God reserves His best medicine for our times of deepest despair."[3]

—L. B. Cowman

DAY FOUR

Equip Against Deception

The world is full of deception, and sometimes it's subtle. An alarm company salesman tried to convince me one Saturday that it would all be free if I signed a contract that day for a new alarm system. I was lured into the trap, falsely believing it was a great deal. Thankfully, I read the contract in detail after he left and quickly realized that none of it was free. I would be locked into a five-year contract, and if I broke it before the five years were up, I would owe them thousands of dollars for the equipment. I was able to cancel without penalty, but I learned a valuable lesson that day about the importance of being alert. Are we equipped to recognize deception? Are we equipping others to be on guard?

Father, I confess I sometimes let my guard down and allow others to deceive me. Give me wisdom on how to avoid it. Keep me alert and sensitive. Thank You for always being with me, equipping me with Your strength to stand against all deception.

Looking to God's Word

2 Timothy 3:13–15

1. *How does Paul describe people in the last days in verse 13?*

2. What does Paul exhort Timothy to do? How is Timothy to live in the middle of deception all around him?

3. How does the Word of God help us fight deception?

4. Timothy's mother and grandmother taught him the sacred writings in his childhood. How can we teach the younger generations the truths of God's Word?

Looking Upward

5. In what ways do we see deception in our world today?

6. What are specific steps we can take to guard against deception?

7. Why are some people still deceived by false teaching even though they have been taught God's Word from an early age? (There are numerous answers for this, but to get you started, look at Ps. 119:9–11 for one possible reason.)

Looking Deeper

8. Paul tells us these men will be deceived and will also deceive others. Read 2 Cor. 11:3. What can we learn about deception from this verse?

Looking Reflectively

We want to trust people and believe what they tell us is true. However, there are some who want to take advantage of us, and we must be equipped to recognize deception in our daily lives, whether in face-to-face relationships or online interactions. In our spiritual lives, we must also be on guard against those who twist the Word of God to deceive us. Paul has emphasized this numerous times in his letter to Timothy. Let's equip ourselves and the generations behind us to stand strong against schemes that would lead us astray from God's truth.

✦ *Ask God to search your heart and show you if you've been deceived in any way.*

✦ *Reflect on Psalm 5. How do David's words encourage you?*

"Each of us is susceptible to this dangerous trap of deception unless we obey Scripture vigilantly. Following Christ is more than a one-time decision or an occasional church service or kind act. True Christianity involves continual dependence and obedience to Christ the king."[4]

—Knute Larson

DAY FIVE

Equip Through God's Word

During my first two years in college, I had my Bible in the dorm room, but I didn't use it. It sat on the shelf, collecting dust. During that time, I drifted away from the Lord and went down a path not pleasing to Him. But once I turned back to Him, I longed for His Word. My friend Bonnie equipped me to study the Bible on my own daily. Scripture gave me courage, strength, and guidance. God wants to equip us for handling life, but how can He if we ignore one of His most essential resources—His Word? If we want to live a life that matters, we must be equipped by spending time in God's Word. Let's equip others to do the same.

Father, I love Your Word. Forgive me for those times I've neglected it. Keep me hungry to be in Your Word every day. Use it to equip me to walk in a manner pleasing to You.

Looking to God's Word

2 Timothy 3:16–17

1. *List all the ways the Word of God is valuable.*

2. How does Scripture lead us to salvation (v. 15)?

3. What does it mean that all Scripture is inspired by God? Why is that significant?

4. How have you seen God's Word to be beneficial for rebuke or correction?

5. How does the Bible correct us? Can you give an example from your own life?

6. How does God's Word train us in righteousness?

7. What is the ultimate goal of Scripture?

Looking Upward

8. Why is it important to spend time in God's Word reading and studying on your own and not just relying on hearing the Word taught by others?

Looking Deeper

9. How does the author of Hebrews describe the Word of God in Hebrews 4:12–13? How does God use His Word in our lives?

Looking Reflectively

A few years ago, I watched a video of Chinese Christians opening a box of Bibles. They grabbed them and held them close to their hearts, crying with joy and giving thanks. Their expressions said it all: Those Bibles were precious to them, and they embraced this gift. How do we respond to our Bibles? Do we hold them tightly and cherish every moment we have in the Word? Do we recognize the gift that the Word of God is to us? May we develop that kind of passion and love for God's Word.

✦ *How devoted are you to spending time in God's Word every day, studying and reading on your own? What can you do to make that time a priority?*

✦ *Meditate on Psalm 119:129–136. Write down your thoughts about God's Word.*

"The purpose of Bible study is not just to understand doctrines or to be able to defend the faith, as important as these things are. The ultimate purpose is the equipping of the believers who read it. It is the Word of God that equips God's people to do the work of God."[5]

—Warren Wiersbe

WEEK SEVEN

Commitment

Are we committed to carrying out our God-given purpose? There will be times when opposition arises, and we'll be tempted to quit. Or we'll face tough times and challenges and say, "I'm done. I'm going to choose an easier path." Sometimes, our fears overshadow our faith, and we lose heart. We need Christian friends who will encourage us to persevere and remain committed to the task God has given us.

Paul faced many hardships and obstacles in his ministry, but he never gave up and walked away. He knew his purpose, and He was committed to carrying out that mission until the end of his earthly journey. He kept his eyes fixed on Jesus.

This week we come to the last part of Paul's final letter to Timothy. In this section, he gives Timothy a powerful charge, exhorting him to fulfill his purpose from God and to be all God designed him to be.

How are you encouraging the younger generations to be committed to their God-given purpose? Are you helping them discover their calling and gifts, and encouraging them to persevere when times get tough? Are you coming alongside them, or are you ignoring them? Are you setting an example that God would want them to follow? Paul did.

Memory Verse: 2 Timothy 4:2. Write the verse below.

DAY ONE

Be Committed to the Lord

Paul encouraged Timothy to stay committed to fulfilling his calling and ministry from the Lord. He continually reminded Timothy of his purpose and how important it was not to get lazy or sidetracked. We all need friends like Paul who will keep us on course. But we also need to be that type of friend to others and encourage them to be all God intended them to be. Are we modeling a commitment to the Lord or the world? Today we'll look at the entire passage for an overview. Ask God to show you how you can grow in your commitment to Him and help others grow in that area.

Father, I desire to follow You wholeheartedly till the day
You take me home. Help me live my life for You.
Convict me when I begin to waver in my commitment.
Keep my focus on You alone.

Looking to God's Word

2 Timothy 4:1–8

1. *What is the authority by which Paul gives Timothy this final charge? Why do you think he included that instead of just telling him what to do?*

2. *List all the imperatives or commands Paul gives Timothy in verses 2 and 5.*

3. *What are the two reasons Paul gives Timothy this specific charge at this time (vv. 3–4, 6)?*

4. *This was a specific exhortation to Timothy in light of his gifting and calling from God. But these instructions can also be applied to us as believers today. We might not have the gift of teaching or preaching, but how can we preach the word in our daily situations?*

Looking Upward

5. If you knew your remaining time on this earth was short, what would you want to say to those you hold dear? What would you encourage them to do with their lives?

Looking Deeper

6. Read 2 Corinthians 5:9–10. What was Paul's ambition in life? What was his motivation?

The *Moody Bible Commentary* gives insight into "the judgment seat of Christ" in verse 10:

> Paul was also motivated by the expectation that he and all Christians will **appear before** and be evaluated by **Christ**. This happens at the **judgment seat** (Gk. *bema*)—a word that referred to a raised platform where a judicial authority pronounced a verdict on the one standing before him. . . . The purpose of the evaluation is not to determine eternal destiny; the purpose is to identify the actions of the physical **body** and to evaluate them as **good** or **bad**. The reward for **good** works is praise (1Co 4:5); the reward for evil works is lack of praise (1Co 3:15).[1]

7. How does it affect your life to know that one day you will stand before the judgment seat of Christ to account for your deeds? Is there something you need to change?

Looking Reflectively

I was with my mom when she took her last breath on this earth, and I pictured Jesus welcoming her home with open arms, saying, "Well done, Marjorie! Well done, good and faithful servant!" Mom lived a life that mattered and left a legacy of eternal significance. None of us wants to get to the end of our lives and stand before God to hear Him say, "I gave you gifts and opportunities, but you didn't use them. I had so much more for you, and you missed it."

John Piper says it well in his book, *Don't Waste Your Life:* "But whatever you do, find the God-centered, Christ-exalting, Bible-saturated passion of your life, and find your way to say it and live for it and die for it. And you will make a difference that lasts. You will not waste your life."[2]

Are we living our lives today in such a way that when we see Him face to face, we'll hear Him say, "Well done, faithful servant"? That's my prayer.

✦ *As you think through your life, how are you investing your time, gifts, and strengths?*

✦ *Write a prayer or psalm to the Lord, expressing your desire to please Him in all areas of your life and make a difference for eternity. Let Hebrews 12:28 guide you.*

"Jesus, today my prayer is that I would be considered trustworthy.
To be so means that I can be trusted to carry out the work you have given me. . . .
Help me to live my life with a full heart, no holding back. . . .
I want my life to be a worshipful offering to you."[3]

—Mary DeMuth

DAY TWO

Be Committed to the Word of God

Paul wanted Timothy to live for the Lord and please Him in every way. As I approach the final chapters of my life on this earth, I've taken time to evaluate how I'm using my time and energy. Am I living each day to the fullest for Him? Is He pleased with how I'm using my gifts? I desire to honor and serve Him, making the most of every day for Him.

Today we'll focus on the charge in 2 Timothy 4:2, where Paul lays out specific exhortations for Timothy. We each have a calling and specific gifts to help us carry out that purpose. Are we committed to fulfilling those tasks for the Lord? Ask God to make you sensitive to the prompting of His Spirit as you look to His Word today.

Father, help me live my life for You, pleasing You in all I do and say. Keep me from becoming complacent about the mission You've given me to carry out. Help me stay focused on You, not the world. I desire to honor You every day of my life.

Looking to God's Word

2 Timothy 4:1–2

1. *Again, list the five imperatives/commands in verse 2.*

2. *What does it mean to be ready "in season"? What does it mean to be ready "out of season"? What would that require?*

3. *What is the difference between correct, rebuke, and exhort? How are they similar?*

4. *How does 4:2 relate to 3:16–17?*

5. Why is it important to do these things with great patience and instruction?

Looking Upward

6. Why are these imperatives important? What difference do they make?

7. How do you know when to correct or rebuke someone and when to remain silent?

Looking Deeper

8. Read Colossians 1:25–29. What does Paul see as his mission/purpose? What was his attitude about it?

9. How does this passage relate to 2 Timothy 4:2?

Looking Reflectively

Paul challenged Timothy to invest his life in others, encouraging them to persevere in their faith. Sometimes that requires rebuking and reproving someone. I admit it's not easy to be on the receiving end, but I realize how vital those words are for my spiritual growth.

During my early years on staff with Cru, I was so busy, striving to prove myself and do my job well. A wise friend pulled me aside one day and gently pointed out that I was operating in my own strength and running myself ragged just to prove my worth. She told me, "You need to slow down and let God work through you (and in you) instead of pushing yourself in your own strength." She was right, and I still think about her words today. I'm so thankful she loved me enough to tell me something needed to change in my life. Will we do the same with those God has placed around us, with gentleness and love?

✦ *How are you speaking God's Word to others? What hinders you in this area?*

✦ *Are you available for God's divine appointments? If not, what needs to change?*

✦ *How are you doing in the areas of giving and receiving correction, rebuke, and exhortation?*

✦ *Pray through Paul's words in Colossians 1:25–29 that we looked at in Looking Deeper.*

"It may be inconvenient to take a stand for Christ or to tell others about his love, but preaching the Word of God is the most important responsibility the church and its members have been given. Be prepared for, courageous in, and sensitive to God-given opportunities to tell the Good News." [4]

—Bruce Barton et al.

DAY THREE

Be Committed to Sound Doctrine

When we're told to do something, we typically want to ask why. If we understand the reason, it can be much easier to accomplish a task that stretches us beyond our comfort zone. Paul didn't just give commands to Timothy in 2 Timothy 4; he also explained why Timothy needed to obey them.

In today's passage, Paul gave the first reason why he exhorted Timothy to "preach the word; be ready in season and out of season; correct, rebuke, and exhort, with great patience and instruction" (2 Tim. 4:2). Paul had already emphasized the importance of following sound doctrine in chapters 1 and 3. Now he returns to that topic here in chapter 4, emphasizing how important sound doctrine is to finishing well. Let's learn from Paul's words and apply them to our lives today.

Lord, there are times I don't always want to do what
Your Word tells me to, especially if it isn't easy.
Help me trust You and accept Your instruction with an open heart.
Make me attentive to those who speak Your Word to me,
trusting they want Your best for me. Keep me teachable.

Looking to God's Word

2 Timothy 4:3–4

1. Why did Paul give these imperatives to Timothy in verse 2?

2. Who do you think "they" are in verses 3–4? Why?

3. What are some reasons why people choose not to listen to sound doctrine?

4. In what ways do we see people wanting to have their ears tickled in our culture now?

5. What are some examples of myths people turn aside to today?

Looking Upward

6. Can you think of a time when someone tried to lead you away from the truth of God's Word? How did you respond?

Looking Deeper

7. Read Colossians 2:8. What is Paul's warning to the Colossian church?

8. What are some examples of philosophy and empty deception that could take us captive?

Looking Reflectively

Many don't regard God's Word as truth and don't consider it relevant, or they twist it to mean what they want it to say. If we're going to make a difference of eternal significance, we must be committed to sound doctrine. (Paul has repeatedly emphasized this in his letter to Timothy.) We have to remain faithful to God's Word and not be subtly drawn away by things that make us feel good or better align with what our culture says is "right." Let's help ground the next generation in God's Word. *Lord, keep us committed to Your Word.*

✦ *Are you in danger of reading, watching, or doing anything that might lure you away from the truth of God's Word? If so, what drew you in?*

✦ *Are you listening—or suspect you may be listening—to someone teaching the Bible incorrectly or interpreting it according to their own desires? If so, why? What should you do?*

✦ *Spend time reflecting on Psalm 119:97–106.*

"There are many 'itching ears,' even within evangelical churches. The itch for 'novelty,' or 'something more' than the sound teaching of the Word of God, has led many to focus on feelings and experience. But feelings are changeable and can never be a firm enough foundation for building up one's spiritual life."[5]

—Peter Williams

DAY FOUR

Be Committed to Ministry

What ministry do you feel God is calling you to? What do you love doing for the Lord? Teaching? Discipling? Encouraging? Coming alongside those in need? Opening your home to others? Organizing? Perhaps you enjoy working with children, teenagers, or senior adults. You may enjoy serving others in tangible ways or have a passion for sharing Christ with anyone who comes across your path.

Paul challenged Timothy to be faithful to his calling. We each have a ministry and calling that God has entrusted to us. Are we committed to our God-given purpose? Will we help the younger generations find their purpose and develop their gifts? This is a vital part of living a life that matters.

Father, thank You for how You've equipped me to serve You.
I don't want to neglect using those gifts You've given me.
Show me how to encourage the generations behind me to discover
their calling and use their gifts to carry it out.
Thank You for allowing me to be a part of Your bigger plan.

Looking to God's Word

2 Timothy 4:5

1. *List Paul's four imperatives/commands to Timothy in this verse.*

2. *Why do you think he instructed Timothy to use self-restraint in all things? What does that mean, and why would that be important?*

3. *Why would Paul exhort Timothy to endure hardship? (See also Paul's charge to Timothy in 2 Tim. 1:8.)*

4. *What is the work of an evangelist?*

5. *What would it look like to fulfill your ministry?*

Looking Upward

6. Is evangelism only to be done by those who have the gift and calling of evangelism? Why or why not?

7. Paul exhorted Timothy to fulfill his ministry. Are you fulfilling your God-given ministry? If not, what is holding you back?

Looking Deeper

8. Read Colossians 4:17. What does Paul say about ministry in his charge to Archippus? What is he to do and why? How did he receive his ministry?

Looking Reflectively

If you haven't already done so, I encourage you to write your personal mission statement. How has God gifted you? Whom has He placed on your heart to serve and come alongside? What energizes you? How can God use your gifts and abilities to carry out that purpose? You can visit my website, **www.crickettkeeth.com**, to download a free document that guides you through a five-step process to develop your personal mission statement.

I was in my forties when a pastor challenged me to sit down and think through my personal mission statement. What did God uniquely design me to do with my life? How was I carrying it out? My mission statement is: *To encourage women to passionately pursue Jesus Christ—through writing, teaching, and discipleship.* That process changed my life. It provided me with direction on where and how to allocate my time. I became aware of what drained me and what energized me and why. It has looked different in how I carry it out in the changing seasons of life, but my purpose hasn't changed.

It's obvious Paul wanted Timothy to be all God created him to be and to carry out the ministry God had entrusted to him. He demonstrated commitment to the Lord in his own ministry and exhorted Timothy to that same commitment. Let's spur one another on to stay faithful to God and what He has called us to do.

✦ ***Consider how you're doing with these four imperatives in 2 Timothy 4:5. What are you doing well, and what do you need to work on?***

"Like Timothy, I want to fully carry out the ministry you have given me. Help me to welcome that ministry instead of running away from it. Reveal a bigger picture of what that means today. Amen."[6]

—Mary DeMuth

DAY FIVE

Be Committed to Finishing Well

God has given each of us a course to run on this earth, a ministry to fulfill. Will we run the course He has laid out for us, or will we forge our own path? I've taken some detours along the way, but I'm so grateful God always pulled me back to where I needed to be. If we desire to live a life that matters—a life of eternal significance—we must run the course He has laid out for each of us uniquely, according to His greater purpose.

As Paul penned this letter to Timothy, he knew he was nearing the end of his journey. He had lived his life in a manner pleasing to God. He was carrying out his God-given purpose and was finishing well. That's my prayer for us—that we'd finish well, pleasing our Master by living a life that makes a difference for His kingdom.

Father, help me finish my journey on this earth well.
Deepen my commitment to carry out Your purpose as long as I'm on this earth.
Protect me from a life of status quo and mediocrity.
May You be pleased and glorified in the way I live my life for You.

Looking to God's Word

2 Timothy 4:6–8

1. *How does Paul describe the way he has lived his life in verses 6–7?*

2. Nelson's New Illustrated Bible Commentary *gives insight about verse 6: "A drink offering was an offering performed by pouring wine out on the ground or altar (Num. 28:11–31)."[7] What do you think Paul meant when he said, "I am already being poured out as a drink offering." (v. 6)? See also Phil. 2:17.*

3. *What helps us fight the good fight in our time on this earth? What weapons and tools are available to us, and how should we use them? Start with reading Ephesians 6.*

4. *What does it mean to keep the faith? What is essential to being able to do that?*

5. What is the connection between loving His appearing and the crown of righteousness (v. 8)? Why would loving His appearing lead to this crown?

6. How is loving His appearing related to fighting the good fight, finishing the course, and keeping the faith?

7. In verse 8, Paul looks forward to his award.

a) What is his award?

b) Who will give it to him?

c) Who is this award for?

d) When will he receive it?

Looking Upward

8. What are some hindrances and obstacles that could make (or have made) you stumble or take a detour? How can you overcome or avoid those obstacles?

Looking Deeper

9. Write 2 Timothy 4:6–8 below. As you do, ponder each word and phrase, and outline the passage.

Looking Reflectively

I don't want to spend the last chapter of my life on this earth just sitting around, waiting for His return. I long to be useful to the Lord until the day He takes me home. But that has to be a daily decision, moment by moment.

In her final years in a nursing home, my mom couldn't speak, hear, walk, or see, but she could smile and grab someone's hand to comfort them. Her smile and encouragement opened the door for me to share about her relationship with Christ. She carried out her purpose till the very end.

Some of you are just starting out on your course with the Lord, and it's still early. But the decisions and choices you make today will influence how you will run the course later. Make wise decisions now that will enable you to finish well.

Others have been running the course for a long time. Some of you are tired and ready to quit, while others remain strong, even though it's difficult. Keep pressing on. Be an example to the next generations of how to finish well.

✦ *If this were your last day (or week) on this earth, how would you sum up your life to this point? What will you be remembered for?*

✦ *How are you making a difference of eternal significance? For example, are you living your life in a way that matters for Christ and His kingdom? Are you investing in material possessions and temporary pleasures, or are you investing in people?*

✦ *Are you living out your God-given purpose, using your spiritual gifts and abilities to serve and honor Him? (This is why it's so essential to develop a personal mission statement. It will help you assess if and how you're carrying out God's purpose. You may want to look back at Week 2, Day 2 of this study, when we discussed being faithful to our calling.)*

David prayed in Psalm 139:23–24: "Search me, God, and know my heart; put me to the test and know my anxious thoughts; and see if there is any hurtful way in me, and lead me in the everlasting way." As I get into bed at night, I often ask God, "Lord, have I pleased you today with my words and actions? If not, show me where I need to change." And He does.

We want to live lives pleasing to the Lord, but we can't in our own strength. We please God as we draw from the power of the Holy Spirit living in us.

"Are you ready to be poured out as an offering?
It is an act of your will, not your emotions.
Tell God you are ready to be offered as a sacrifice for Him.
Then accept the consequences as they come, without any complaints,
in spite of what God may send your way."[8]

—Oswald Chambers

WEEK EIGHT

Steadfastness

For several years, my family would gather at the beach for a week of vacation each summer. One of my cherished memories from that time was the image of seagulls lined up on the shore. They stood at attention, with their faces to the wind, determined that no storm would knock them over. That image would always bring to mind the word *steadfast*. And I would pray, *Lord, I want to be steadfast like those seagulls when the storms and winds come, standing strong and unwavering regardless of what comes at me.*

Paul has given Timothy his final words of encouragement and exhortation as he nears his departure to his heavenly home. He has lived a life that matters, making a difference in the lives of many for Christ. Some started well but didn't finish strong, while others remained steadfast to God's Word and encouraged Paul during difficult times. Paul faced his share of storms in his life, but he stood steadfast, keeping his eyes on Jesus. As a result, he finished well.

And that should be our goal. This final section of Paul's letter to Timothy encourages us to stand steadfast, no matter what storms we may face.

Memory verse: 2 Timothy 4:18. Write it below.

DAY ONE

Stand Steadfast When Relationships Disappoint

Difficult relationships are part of life. People will let us down when we need them most, speak unkind words, or walk away when the going gets tough. Some will choose to follow their own path and listen to the world instead of God's leading. Don't become discouraged, but learn from the situation and let it draw you into a deeper intimacy with God. Remain steadfast in your faith and pray for steadfastness in others.

Today, we'll focus on two disappointing and difficult relationships in Paul's life. Ask God to teach you through Paul's situation how to stand strong when others let you down or oppose you.

Father, we've all had relationships that have hurt or disappointed us. With some, I can see how You used that pain for good to draw me into a deeper love for You. Thank You that I can trust You with all my relationships—the good and the hard. Give me strength and guidance to respond in a godly way to those relationships that are not easy.

Looking to God's Word

2 Timothy 4:9–15

1. *Paul begins this section by mentioning Demas and his lack of steadfastness. According to verse 10, what was Demas's stumbling block, and what was the result?*

2. *What characteristics would indicate that someone loves this present world?*

3. *How does loving this world hinder one's walk with God?*

4. *Alexander was also mentioned in a negative light. What do we learn about Alexander in verses 14–15?*

5. What do Paul's words in verse 14, "the Lord will repay him according to his deeds," reveal about Paul's heart and his relationship with God?

Looking Upward

6. Why would someone choose to love this present world over God?

7. In what ways do people oppose the teaching of God's Word today?

Looking Deeper

8. Demas, at one point, was helpful to Paul. What do we learn about Demas in Colossians 4:14 and Philemon 23–24?

Looking Reflectively

I've had my share of disappointing relationships in life—those who have opposed me in sharing the gospel, those who have talked negatively about me, and friends who have not stayed steadfast in their walk with God. It's hard, but God continues to remind me that He's in control and has a purpose for everything that happens. Nothing touches my life that isn't allowed by God.

When someone disappoints or hurts us, we can either get angry and lash out at them in revenge, or we can entrust them into God's hands, asking God to work His purpose in and through them. Let's ask God for strength to respond in a way that honors Him.

✦ *Reflect on the words of David in Psalm 9:9–10. How do his words encourage you today?*

✦ *How has someone hurt or disappointed you? Are you struggling to let it go and move on? Draw from the power of the Holy Spirit and follow the example of Paul. Forgive and leave them in God's hands.*

✦ *Is there someone you've disappointed or let down you need to ask forgiveness from?*

"Dear Jesus, thank You for the hardship, heartbreak, and hopelessness we feel in this life; they remind us that You really are our only Hope. Hold us close today. Warm our hearts as we remember that You never let us go. In Jesus's name, amen."[1]

—Cleere Cherry

DAY TWO

Stand Steadfast With Encouraging Relationships (Part 1)

During my years of working in full-time ministry, one of the areas I have loved most is being part of a team. I'm not a lone ranger, and I need others who fill in the gaps of my weaknesses. It's helpful (and fun) to have a group to brainstorm and work hand in hand with as we seek to minister to others. Together, we can accomplish more for the Lord than we can by going it alone. That's also true for our spiritual walk. We need a team to come alongside and push us forward when we become discouraged or want to quit, as well as redirect us when we're getting off course.

Paul made a difference in countless lives as he served the Lord Jesus Christ. He didn't attempt to serve the Lord solo but invited others to join him. He knew the importance of teamwork and training others for ministry. He also had a team of people who supported and encouraged him in his ministry. Today we get a glimpse into the lives of some of Paul's teammates.

Father, thank You for the encouragers and teammates You've brought into my life over the years. Thank You for how they have motivated me in my walk with You and helped me stand steadfast in stormy times. Use me to encourage others in their relationship with You.

Looking to God's Word and Looking Deeper

2 Timothy 4:9–13

1. *List the names of those Paul mentioned in a positive way.*

2. *Crescens is only mentioned in 2 Timothy 4:10. What is implied about him by Paul's comment, "Crescens has gone to Galatia"?*

3. *Paul refers to Titus in verse 10. What additional information do we learn about Titus from these passages below? How was Titus used by God to work alongside Paul in the ministry?*

   2 Corinthians 7:6–7

   "But God, who comforts the discouraged, comforted us by the arrival of Titus; and not only by his arrival, but also by the comfort with which he was comforted among you, as he reported to us your longing, your mourning, your zeal for me; so that I rejoiced even more."

2 Corinthians 8:16–17, 23

"But thanks be to God who puts the same earnestness in your behalf in the heart of Titus. For he not only accepted our appeal, but being himself very earnest, he has gone to you of his own accord. . . . As for Titus, he is my partner and fellow worker among you; as for our brothers, they are messengers of the churches, a glory to Christ."

Titus 1:4–5

"To Titus, my true son in a common faith: Grace and peace from God the Father and Christ Jesus our Savior. For this reason I left you in Crete, that you would set in order what remains and appoint elders in every city as I directed you."

4. *Only Luke was with Paul at this time (v. 11). Acts 16 points out that Luke had joined Paul for part of his second missionary journey. We looked at two passages in Looking Deeper yesterday that mentioned Luke along with Demas. What else do we learn about Luke from the introduction in his letter to Theophilus in Luke 1:1–4?*

Luke 1:1–4

"Since many have undertaken to compile an account of the things accomplished among us, just as they were handed down to us by those who from the beginning were eyewitnesses and servants of the word, it seemed fitting to me as well, having investigated everything carefully from the beginning, to write it out for you in an orderly sequence, most excellent Theophilus; so that you may know the exact truth about the things you have been taught."

5. *What items did Paul want Timothy to bring him (v. 13)? Why do you think he wanted these items?*

6. *In light of Acts 15:36–41 (read below), why are Paul's comments about Mark significant in 2 Timothy 4:11?*

   Acts 15:36–41

   "After some days Paul said to Barnabas, 'Let's return and visit the brothers and sisters in every city in which we proclaimed the word of the Lord, and see how they are.' Barnabas wanted to take John, called Mark, along with them also. But Paul was of the opinion that they should not take along with them this man who had deserted them in Pamphylia and had not gone with them to the work. Now it turned into such a sharp disagreement that they separated from one another, and Barnabas took Mark with him and sailed away to Cyprus. But Paul chose Silas, and left after being entrusted by the brothers to the grace of the Lord. And he was traveling through Syria and Cilicia, strengthening the churches."

7. *Paul sent Tychicus to Ephesus (v. 12). What do you learn about Tychicus from these passages? How was he useful to Paul in the ministry?*

   Ephesians 6:21–22

   "Now, so that you also may know about my circumstances as to what I am doing, Tychicus, the beloved brother and faithful servant in the Lord, will make everything known to you. I have sent him to you for this very purpose, so that you may know about us, and that he may comfort your hearts."

Colossians 4:7–9

"As to all my affairs, Tychicus, our beloved brother and faithful servant and fellow bond-servant in the Lord, will bring you information. For I have sent him to you for this very purpose, that you may know about our circumstances and that he may encourage your hearts; and with him is Onesimus, our faithful and beloved brother, who is one of your own. They will inform you about the whole situation here."

Looking Upward

8. As you learn about these five men, what stands out to you?

9. Do you tend to be more of a lone ranger in ministry, or do you like working with teams? Why?

Looking Reflectively

People come and go in our lives. Some help shape us for the better. Others can be challenging, and sometimes they disappoint us. But we can be confident that God places people in our lives for a purpose.

I'm grateful for the women God has brought into my life to serve together with—whether in the local church, in the city, or on a mission trip abroad. It's been a joy to watch God bring teams together, each member contributing their unique gifts for a common purpose—making Jesus known and discipling new believers. Yes, there are conflicts at times, but God is at work as we walk through life together.

✦ *Who is on your team of encouragers and co-laborers?*

✦ *In what areas can you model steadfastness today?*

✦ *How are you serving alongside the body of Christ? How are you encouraging others in ministry? In their personal lives?*

✦ ***Write out Hebrews 10:23–25. What should we be doing? How does this passage relate to being steadfast?***

"This is the only mention of Crescens (whose name means "growing") in the Bible. We know nothing more about him. This should be an encouragement to all believers. No matter how humble their position in life may be, even an errand run for the Lord will not go unnoticed or unrewarded."[2]

—William MacDonald

DAY THREE

Stand Steadfast When You Feel Alone

It's important to have Christian friends in our lives who encourage us in our faith and stand beside us when we feel weak. God designed us for community in the body of Christ. Going it alone can be hard and dangerous for our spiritual walk, but sometimes God places us in situations where we are alone and away from our Christian friends for a time.

Life had its ups and downs for Paul. He had great friends and coworkers who came alongside him and supported him in the ministry, but he also had those who opposed him or turned away from the Lord and disappointed him. There were also times when Paul was alone, and his friends were elsewhere. But Paul knew where his strength and confidence lay—not in people, but in God. Today's passage provides a snapshot of a season in Paul's life when he felt abandoned and all alone.

When you feel alone, disappointed, and discouraged, where do you turn? Will you stay steadfast in your faith?

Father, thank You that I can run to You when people disappoint me or are not there when I need them. Thank You for always being faithful. You will never desert or forsake me. Hold me close in those times I feel abandoned. Remind me that Your presence is enough.

Looking to God's Word

2 Timothy 4:16–18

1. *In verse 16, Paul shares his heart. How was he feeling at this point?*

Paul mentions his "first defense." *Nelson's New Testament Survey* gives insight into what he was probably referring to here: "It was customary under Roman law for accused prisoners to have a preliminary hearing before their trial. At this hearing, witnesses could speak on behalf of the accused. In Paul's case no one had come to his defense."[3]

2. *What are some possible reasons why no one came to his defense?*

3. *What do Paul's words in verse 16, "may it not be counted against them," imply about Paul's heart and the way he was handling this disappointment?*

4. *How does Paul express his confidence in God during this difficult time? List all that Paul said God did or will do for him.*

5. What does Paul see as God's purpose for him in this situation (v. 17)? How did he see God at work through this?

Paul stated that he was "rescued out of the lion's mouth" in verse 17. There are different interpretations of what this means. Some believe he is referring to Nero and being protected from death at his first preliminary trial. Others think this is referring to Satan and the spiritual battle. He goes on to say in verse 18, "The Lord will rescue me from every evil deed."

6. What do you think he means here and why?

Looking Upward

7. Even though Paul felt abandoned and alone, he could still praise God (v. 18). How was he (and how are we) able to praise God in the middle of discouraging circumstances?

8. How has the Lord strengthened you in trials? What helps you walk through seasons when you feel alone and deserted by friends?

Looking Deeper

9. Read Psalm 118:1–9. How did David respond when he was in distress? How did he find his strength in God and stay steadfast in the Lord?

Looking Reflectively

Paul could have finished his life blaming God for allowing him to be put in prison and on trial. He could have become bitter toward those who hurt and abandoned him. But he didn't. Instead, he ended this letter by praising God in verse 18: "To Him be the glory forever and ever. Amen." Paul was steadfast in his faith to the very end.

Even though Paul's friends and coworkers were not there to support him, he was confident he was not alone. God was with him every step of the way, and he knew his strength came from God.

Are you feeling alone and deserted today? Turn to the Lord. He is always with you. Draw from His strength and find comfort in His presence.

✦ *Spend some time in prayer. Be honest with how you're feeling. What verses strengthen you today? (I love Psalm 73:23–26.)*

"Paul's courage in proclaiming the gospel was not dampened by the weakness of those around him. The secret to his ministry was his dependence on the strength of God."[4]

—Duane Litfin

DAY FOUR

Stand Steadfast with Encouraging Relationships (Part 2)

Paul made a difference of eternal significance after coming to faith in Christ. He dedicated his life to leading people to Jesus and helping them grow in their relationship with God. And he was willing to endure hardship to accomplish his purpose. In Day 2's lesson this week, we examined five men Paul mentioned as coworkers for the gospel. Today, we'll continue focusing on a few others he mentioned at the end of the letter who were engaged in ministry with him.

Paul surrounded himself with a team of people and fellow ministers wherever he went. And he was willing to send them out to work in new areas, even if that meant he would be alone. What a great example to follow as we seek to stand steadfast in serving God.

Father, thank You for the example of Paul and how he served You wholeheartedly. I desire to be committed like Paul to helping others serve and grow deeper in their walk with You. Use me to help equip others to carry out Your mission.

Looking to God's Word

2 Timothy 4:19–22

1. List each name Paul mentions in these verses.

2. What do we learn about Prisca (Priscilla) and Aquila (v. 19) and their relationship with Paul from these verses below?

Acts 18:1–3

"After these events Paul left Athens and went to Corinth. And he found a Jew named Aquila, a native of Pontus having recently come from Italy with his wife Priscilla, because Claudius had commanded all the Jews to leave Rome. He came to them, and because he was of the same trade he stayed with them, and they worked together, for they were tent-makers by trade."

Acts 18:18

"Now Paul, when he had remained many days longer, took leave of the brothers and sisters and sailed away to Syria, and Priscilla and Aquila were with him."

Romans 16:3–4

"Greet Prisca and Aquila, my fellow workers in Christ Jesus, who risked their own necks for my life, to whom not only do I give thanks, but also all the churches of the Gentiles."

3. Onesiphorus (v. 19) and Paul had an endearing relationship. What do we learn about him from 2 Timothy 1:16–18?

4. In verse 20, Paul tells us that Erastus remained at Corinth. What else do we know about Erastus from Acts 19:22?

Acts 19:22

"And after he sent into Macedonia two of those who assisted him, Timothy and Erastus, he himself stayed in Asia for a while."

5. Verse 20 also states that Paul left Trophimus sick at Miletus. What else do we learn about Trophimus from Acts 20:4? What is notable about this group of men with Paul? Why would that be significant?

Acts 20:4

"And he was accompanied by Sopater of Berea, the son of Pyrrhus, and by Aristarchus and Secundus of the Thessalonians, and Gaius of Derbe, and Timothy, and Tychicus and Trophimus of Asia."

Looking Upward

6. Paul mentions several other people by name in verse 21, but we don't know anything about them other than Paul thinks fondly of them. What stands out about the people Paul mentioned in this chapter and their relationships with Paul?

Looking Deeper

7. Paul had a deep love for all the churches he worked with. As you read his words to the Thessalonian church in 1 Thessalonians 2:7–13, describe his relationship with them. How did he love and serve them?

8. Why did he invest his life in them (v. 12)?

Looking Reflectively

Several years ago, I attended a memorial service that lasted over three hours! There was testimony after testimony from people of all ages and places who had been spiritually impacted by this woman's life. She demonstrated steadfastness in her walk with God and how to finish well. No, she didn't leave behind a large sum of money or property, but she left a legacy of eternal significance. She changed many lives (including mine), drawing people into a deeper relationship with God. She lived a life that mattered—a life that made a difference for eternity.

Paul, too, had a far-reaching impact beyond any one city or generation. He built into the lives of brothers and sisters in Christ to multiply the gospel throughout the nations. We may not see now how God is using us as we build into the lives of others through discipleship and mentoring, but one day, we will. Stay steadfast!

✦ *How can you spur someone on to stay steadfast in their faith today?*

✦ *Ponder the words of Paul to the Corinthians in 1 Corinthians 15:58. What did Paul encourage them to do? Why? How can you apply this message in your life today?*

✦ *Take time to thank God for those you are serving alongside and for those who have built into your life.*

Who are you building into today to help them become more like Christ? If you're looking for someone to mentor/disciple, ask God to bring that person across your path. Be available.

"How I thank the Lord for people in my life like Onesiphorus—dear friends whose encouraging words and acts have ministered much-needed grace to my heart and have helped me to stay the course and press into the battle. Thinking about those people motivates me to reach out to others around me who may be in need of refreshing and comfort from Christ."[5]

—Nancy DeMoss Wolgemuth

DAY FIVE

Review and Reflection

We have completed our study of the book of 2 Timothy and learned how Paul lived a life that mattered as he invested in the lives of Timothy and so many others. He left a legacy of eternal significance.

This is a good time to reflect on how we're living our lives. Are you investing in things that are only temporary—material possessions, wealth, success? Or are you making a difference for God's kingdom by investing in others and helping them grow and develop in their walk with God? Are you living a life that matters for eternity or one that will be quickly forgotten or remembered in a negative light? Are you finishing the course God has given you to run?

I pray we will live every day for Christ, fulfilling His purpose for us and helping others live out their God-given purpose. As we conclude our study of 2 Timothy, let's review this final letter Paul wrote Timothy and note the lessons we want to apply in our lives.

Father, thank You for the example of Paul and how he made a difference by building into the lives of others, equipping them to follow and serve You. I want to do the same. Keep me from getting distracted by the world. I want to honor You with my life.

Looking to God's Word

1. *What verses especially encouraged you or convicted you from this letter?*

2. *What did you learn about God?*

3. *What did you learn about the Christian life? About yourself?*

4. *Are there warnings or exhortations that hit close to home for you? How can you avoid these dangers?*

Looking Upward

5. Paul encouraged Timothy and exhorted him to finish well. What are you doing to finish well?

6. Is there something you need to change?

Looking Deeper

7. Read John 17:4. How do Jesus' words to the Father motivate you in how you live your life?

Looking Reflectively

Paul challenged Timothy and all believers to leave a legacy of eternal significance. You're never too young to begin. Don't wait till you're in your later years. Ask God to make you usable right where you are in the season He has you. And if you're in the final chapter of your life, be available to God until the day He takes you home. He has not put you on a shelf. Your ministry may look different from what it did in your earlier years, but God is still at work in and through you. Make every day count for Him.

When I reach the end of my life, I want to be able to say as Paul did in 2 Timothy 4:7: "I've fought the good fight, I have finished the course, I have kept the faith." May this be true for each one of us.

✦ ***As you reflect on these eight qualities in Paul's life, which ones are demonstrated in your life and how? Which qualities do you need to work on?***

✦ *Write out the benediction from Hebrews 13:20–21 below. Make this your prayer for yourself and others as you strive to finish well.*

"The Bible does not record the final days of Paul.
Tradition tells us that he was found guilty and sentenced to die.
He was probably taken outside the city and beheaded.
But Timothy and the other devoted believers carried on the work! . . .
You and I must be faithful so that (if the Lord does not return soon)
future generations may hear the Gospel and have the opportunity to be saved."[6]

—Warren Wiersbe

Leader's Guide

Regardless of your stage in life, I pray that you will choose to live a life that matters—a life of eternal significance. Learn from Paul's example in 2 Timothy. He didn't leave behind wealth or material possessions, but he left behind a legacy of people who would continue his ministry to make Jesus known.

This study can be used individually or with a small group. I took my women through this study right before I retired as the women's ministry director at my church, wanting to give them a final charge for their lives. I provided the leaders with direction each week on which questions to discuss with their small groups. This guide is a result of that time with my small group leaders. Try to answer the questions on your own first, even if you're unsure how to respond. Then, refer to this guide for clarification and insight.

In your small groups, don't try to discuss every question. Choose several questions each day primarily from the Looking to God's Word and Looking Upward sections, depending on how much time you have in small groups. Be sure to cover questions from all five days. I encourage you to circle the questions you'd like to ask as you first go through the study on your own. Which ones would promote rich discussion and help impart the main message of the lesson that day? I'll recommend questions in this guide, but feel free to use the questions you feel would be most helpful to your group.

The Looking Deeper questions cover other passages that enhance the study but aren't focused on the main passage of that day. In the small group times, I don't usually ask the Looking Deeper questions unless someone has a specific question about them.

Some of the Looking to God's Word questions are straightforward, and you're answering directly from the passage. You don't need to ask those questions. You can just summarize the answer (or ask someone in the small group to do so). Spend your time in small group focusing on the questions that are more open-ended and would best facilitate sharing and discussion.

In this Leader's Guide, I highlight the questions that would promote discussion and address some of the more challenging questions. You can also access the SoundCloud recordings or watch the video lectures for this study for free on my website: https://www.crickettkeeth.com/teaching.

Week One: Encouragement

Day One: Overview of the Letter

Review the setting, Discuss questions 1, 2, 6, and the application question in Looking Reflectively.

Day Two: Encouragement Through Words of Greeting

Discuss questions 2, 3, 5, and 6.

Day Three: Encouragement Through Relationships

Discuss questions 2, 4, 5, and 6.

2. Paul stated in verse 3 that he served God with a "clear conscience." What do you think that means? What leads to a clear conscience?

His motives were pure. He served to honor and glorify God, not for selfish gain. He wasn't hiding anything. Also, he knew he was forgiven for his past and cleansed by the blood of Christ. He didn't need to live with guilt. He could live wholeheartedly to serve and honor Christ, without dwelling on his past. (The Scriptures in Question 3 help answer this question.)

4. Who are the "forefathers" Paul referred to in 2 Timothy 1:3?

He was probably referring to the patriarchs of his Jewish faith (Israel).

Day Four: Encouragement Through Affirmation

Summarize question 1. Discuss any of the questions 2, 4, 5, 6, 7, or 8.

4. What is the "gift of God" that Paul mentioned in verse 6? Read 1 Timothy 4:12–14 for additional insight.

Some say the gift is a special endowment given to Timothy to carry out his ministry. However, I agree with Warren Wiersbe's explanation: "Paul reminded Timothy of the time God called him into service and the local church ordained him. Paul had laid his hands on Timothy (1 Tim. 4:14). Through Paul, God had imparted to Timothy the spiritual gift he needed for his ministry. The laying on of hands was a common practice in apostolic days (Acts 6:6; 13:3), but no believer today has the same authority and privileges that the apostles did. Today, when we lay hands on people for the ministry, it is a symbolic act and does not necessarily impart any special spiritual gifts to them."[1]

Today, we receive our spiritual gifts from the Holy Spirit when we put our faith in Christ as Savior (1 Cor. 12:11).

5. Paul reminded Timothy to "kindle afresh the gift of God." What do you think that means? How would someone go about doing this?

Determine what your gifts are. Don't ignore them. Use them. Don't let them go to waste.

6. What are some possible reasons why Paul would need to remind Timothy of this?

Perhaps he was scared of persecution and did not want to use his gifts and draw attention to himself as a Christian. Also, he may have quit using his gifts because Paul wasn't with him physically in Ephesus at the time.

7. Do you know what your spiritual gifts are? How do we determine what they are?

Try different things and see what you're passionate about. What do you love to do, and what do you do well? What energizes you? Ask people who know you well what they believe your gifts are.

Day Five: Encouragement Through Exhortation

Discuss any of the questions 2–7.

Week Two: Faithfulness

Day One: Be Faithful to Suffer Well

Discuss questions 1, 3, 5, and 6.

Day Two: Be Faithful to Your Calling

Discuss questions 1–4. Summarize question 5. Ask several to share their answer to questions 6 and 7.

Day Three: Be Faithful to Know Your Savior

Discuss questions 1, 2, 4, 5, 6, 7, and 8.

5. Paul said in verse 12, "I am convinced that He is able to protect what I have entrusted to Him until that day." Commentators are divided on what it is that Paul has entrusted to Him. Some think he's referring to his salvation. Others see it as the gospel. Another view is Paul's life and his ministry. Do you have another idea? What do you think Paul is referring to and why?

The Moody Bible Commentary gives this insight: "Some think this refers to Paul's salvation. Others see it as a reference to the gospel or to Paul's ministry. But what is entrusted in this verse belongs to Paul rather than God, indicating that it refers to his life or ministry."[2]

6. What and when is "that day" Paul refers to in this verse? Read 1 Corinthians 1:7–8 and 2 Timothy 4:8. What insight do these passages give?

The day we see Jesus face-to-face (either at His return or when He takes us home)

Day Four: Be Faithful to Sound Doctrine

Summarize question 1. Discuss any of the questions 2–7.

4. What is the treasure Paul is referring to in verse 14? What insight does the New Living Translation (NLT) give? "Through the power of the Holy Spirit who lives within us, carefully guard the precious truth that has been entrusted to you."

Most scholars agree that Paul is referring to the truth of the gospel that has been entrusted to them to share with others.

5. What does it mean to protect or guard through the Holy Spirit the treasure that has been entrusted to you (v. 14)?

Keep the Word pure. Don't change it or water it down. Stay true to sound doctrine. Ask the Holy Spirit to convict you when you're getting off track.

Day Five: Be Faithful to Others

Discuss questions 1, 4, 5, 6, and 7.

Week Three: Strength

Day One: Overview

Discuss questions 1, 2, 3, and 5.

Day Two: Be Strong in Teaching Others

Discuss questions 1, 2, 4, 5, and 6.

Day Three: Be Strong Like a Soldier

Discuss questions 2, 3, 5, 6, and 7.

Day Four: Be Strong Like an Athlete and Farmer

Discuss questions 1, 2, 3, 5, and 6.

Day Five: Be Strong Like Jesus

Discuss questions 1, 3, 4, and 7.

4. What do you think Paul meant when he said, "the word of God is not imprisoned" (v. 9)?

God's Word will go out and accomplish its purpose, no matter how difficult the circumstances. It cannot be contained or restricted.

Week Four: Diligence

Day One: Be Diligent to Guard Your Words

Discuss questions 2, 3, 4, 6, and 7.

7. Some things, like the non-negotiables of the faith, are worth standing up for and defending. What are some non-negotiables of our Christian faith?

Salvation by faith alone, in Jesus alone—not by works; eternal security; Jesus is God, and part of the Trinity; the inspiration and authority of Scripture; He will return one day.

Day Two: Be Diligent to Handle God's Word Accurately

Discuss questions 2, 3, 5, and 6.

5. Paul exhorts Timothy to "avoid worldly and empty chatter" (v. 16). He's not talking about gossip or slander here. What do you think he's referring to in light of verse 18?

Things that are contrary to God's Word and are of no benefit to the hearer to help him grow deeper with Christ.

Day Three: Be Diligent to Abstain from Wickedness

Discuss questions 2, 4, 5, and 6.

Day Four: Be Diligent to Be an Implement for Honor

Discuss questions 1, 2, and 5.

1. What do you think the large house in verse 20 represents in light of verse 19?

The church, the body of Christ

Day Five: Be Diligent to Pursue Becoming Like Christ

Discuss questions 2, 3, 4, 7, and 8.

Week Five: Vigilance

Day One: Be Vigilant in the Last Days

Discuss questions 2, 3, 4, 5, and 6.

Day Two: Be Vigilant Against Loving Self

Discuss questions 1, 2, 3, 6, 7, and 8.

Day Three: Be Vigilant Against Ungodly Attitudes

Discuss questions 1, 3, 4, and 5.

Day Four: Be Vigilant Against Ungodly Actions

Discuss questions 2, 3, and 4.

2. The final characteristic he mentions is "holding to a form of godliness, although they have denied its power" (v. 5). What do you think that means? How do we see that today?

Warren Wiersbe explains it well in his commentary: "Paul stated that these people he has just described would consider themselves religious! "Having a form of godliness" (2 Tim. 3:5) suggests an outward appearance of religion, not true Christian faith; for they have never experienced the power of God in their lives. Form without force. Religion without reality."[3]

3. *Paul instructs Timothy to "avoid such people as these" in verse 5. What did he mean? How do we do that and still reach out to those who need Christ?*

Some believe he was referring to the false teachers in the church, and that Timothy was to avoid them and their teaching. Others take the view that Timothy is not to spend time with them in their godless activities, but only for the purpose of evangelism.

Day Five: Be Vigilant Toward the World

Discuss questions 2, 3, 5, 6, and 7.

5. *What does it mean by "always learning and never able to come to the knowledge of the truth" in verse 7?*

Hearing the Word taught, but not applying it in their lives; hearing the gospel and perhaps professing to be a Christian but not accepting Christ.

Week Six: Equipping

Day One: Equip by Example

Summarize question 1. Discuss any of the questions 3–7.

Day Two: Equip for Suffering

Discuss questions 2, 3, 4, and 5.

Day Three: Equip to Suffer Well

Combine questions 1–2 and 4–5. Discuss question 6.

Day Four: Equip Against Deception

Summarize questions 1 and 2. Discuss questions 3, 5, and 7.

Day Five: Equip Through God's Word

Discuss questions 2, 3, 4, 6, and 8.

Week Seven: Commitment

Day One: Be Committed to the Lord

Discuss questions 1, 4, 5, and 7.

Day Two: Be Committed to the Word of God

Discuss questions 2, 3, 5, and 7.

Day Three: Be Committed to Sound Doctrine

Discuss questions 3, 4, and 5.

Day Four: Be Committed to Ministry

Discuss questions 2, 5, 6, and 7.

6. Is evangelism only to be done by those who have the gift and calling of evangelism? Why or why not?

No. We're all called to be witnesses for Christ and share the gospel (Mark 16:15 and Acts 1:8). But those who have the gift of evangelism are always looking for opportunities to share the gospel and tend to be bolder than those who don't have the gift. They are always looking for an opportunity to share the gospel in any setting. But we all can share Christ in some way with those God puts in our path.

Day Five: Be Committed to Finishing Well

Discuss any of the questions 2–6.

Week Eight: Steadfastness

Day One: Stand Steadfast When Relationships Disappoint

Review question 1. Discuss questions 2, 3, 5, 6, and 7.

Day Two: Stand Steadfast With Encouraging Relationships (Part 1)

Discuss questions 8 and 9.

Day Three: Stand Steadfast When You Feel Alone

Discuss any of these questions.

Day Four: Stand Steadfast With Encouraging Relationships (Part 2)

Discuss question 6.

Day Five: Review and Reflection

Discuss any of these questions. Encourage your women to share a takeaway from 2 Timothy that they want to apply in their lives.

Acknowledgments

My deepest gratitude to:

My Lord and Savior Jesus Christ—for loving me and giving Your life for me. I want to live a life that matters for You and Your kingdom.

The women who have discipled and mentored me throughout my life—for making a difference of eternal significance.

First Evangelical Church in Memphis—for your encouragement and support for my writing and teaching.

Sandra Glahn, Sue Edwards, Joye Baker (my mentors at Dallas Theological Seminary)—for spurring me on to carry out the ministry God entrusted me with.

Cynthia Ruchti, my agent—for your perseverance and wisdom in helping me navigate the publishing world and refine my writing.

Judy Dunagan, my first acquisitions editor and kindred spirit—for believing in me and this Bible study. Thank you for your encouragement along the way.

Erin Davis, my new acquisitions editor—for encouraging and walking alongside me on this journey.

Amanda Cleary Eastep, my developmental editor—for your encouragement, guidance, and expertise in helping make this study far better than what I started with.

The entire Moody Publishers team—for guiding me step by step through this process and getting this study into the hands of others. You are all a delight to work with!

My writing buddies (you know who you are)—for encouraging and praying for me. You understand the ups and downs of writing and know how to pray and encourage.

Notes

Week One: Encouragement

1. Mark Bailey et al., *Nelson's New Testament Survey: Discover the Background, Theology and Meaning of Every Book in the New Testament* (Word, 1999), 477.
2. Bruce B. Barton, David Veerman, and Neil S. Wilson, "1 Timothy, 2 Timothy, Titus," in *Life Application Bible Commentary* (Tyndale House Publishers, 1993), 144.
3. John F. MacArthur, "2 Timothy," in *MacArthur New Testament Commentary* (Moody, 1995), 2.
4. J. Oswald Sanders, *Spiritual Leadership* (Moody, 2007), 40.
5. Rachael Adams, *A Little Goes a Long Way: 52 Days to a Significant Life* (BroadStreet Publishing Group, 2022), 120.
6. Philip Towner, "1–2 Timothy & Titus," vol. 14 in *The IVP New Testament Commentary Series* (InterVarsity Press, 1994), 2 Ti 1:3–5.
7. R. Kent Hughes and Bryan Chapell, "1 & 2 Timothy and Titus: To Guard the Deposit," in *Preaching the Word* (Crossway Books, 2000), 172–173.

Week Two: Faithfulness

1. Carolyn Custis James, *When Life and Beliefs Collide* (Zondervan, 2001), 79.
2. Maggie Wallem Rowe, *This Life We Share* (NavPress, 2020), 64.
3. William MacDonald, *Believer's Bible Commentary: Old and New Testaments*, ed. Arthur Farstad (Thomas Nelson Publishers, 1995), 2112.
4. Earl D. Radmacher, Ronald Barclay Allen, and H. Wayne House, *Nelson's New Illustrated Bible Commentary* (Thomas Nelson Publishers, 1999), 1611.

5. Nancy DeMoss Wolgemuth, *The Quiet Place: Daily Devotional Readings* (Moody, 2012), June 2.

Week Three: Strength

1. Paul David Tripp, *New Morning Mercies: A Daily Gospel Devotional* (Crossway, 2014), Jan. 12.
2. Warren W. Wiersbe, *Wiersbe's Expository Outlines on the New Testament* (Victor Books, 1992), 645.
3. Gary W. Demarest and Lloyd J. Ogilvie, "1, 2 Thessalonians / 1, 2 Timothy / Titus," vol. 32 in *The Preacher's Commentary Series* (Thomas Nelson, 1984), 261.
4. Barton et al., *Life Application Bible Commentary*, 182.
4. Lucinda Secrest McDowell, *Life-Giving Choices* (New Hope Publishers, 2019), 58.

Week Four: Diligence

1. Michael Martin, *Explore the Bible: Adult Commentary: 1 & 2 Timothy, Titus (Spring 2013): Entrusted with God's Good News* (LifeWay Christian Resources, 2013), 87.
2. Nancy DeMoss Wolgemuth, *Revive My Heart: A Year of Daily Reflections* (Moody, 2023), October 5.
3. Tom Constable, *Tom Constable's Expository Notes on the Bible* (Galaxie Software, 2003), 2 Ti 2:19.
4. J. Vernon McGee, *Thru the Bible Commentary*, electronic ed., vol. 5 (Thomas Nelson, 1997), 468.
5. Lawrence O. Richards, *The Bible Reader's Companion*, electronic ed. (Victor Books, 1991), 842.
6. Hughes and Chapell, *Preaching the Word*, 219.

Week Five: Vigilance

1. Lucinda Secrest McDowell, *Ordinary Graces* (Abingdon Press, 2017), 242.
2. Charles R. Swindoll, *Rise & Shine: A Wake-up Call* (Multnomah, 1989), 152.
3. George W. Knight, "1-2 Timothy/Titus," in *Evangelical Commentary on the Bible*, vol. 3, Baker Reference Library (Baker Book House, 1995), 1113.
4. John R. W. Stott, "Guard the Gospel the Message of 2 Timothy" in *The Bible Speaks Today* (InterVarsity Press, 1973), 86.
5. Peter Williams, *Opening up 2 Timothy* (Day One Publications, 2007), 70.

6. Oswald Chambers, *My Utmost for His Highest Updated Edition* (Discovery House, 1992), June 5.

Week Six: Equipping

1. Luther Dorr, *Explore the Bible: Adult Commentary:1 and 2 Timothy, Titus* (Lifeway Christian Resources, 2004), 95–96.
2. Jerry Bridges, *Trusting God* (NavPress, 2008), 95.
3. L. B. Cowman, Updated by Jim Reimann, *Streams in the Desert: 366 Daily Devotional Readings* (Zondervan, 2008), May 10.
4. Knute Larson, "I & II Thessalonians, I & II Timothy, Titus, Philemon," vol. 9 in *Holman New Testament Commentary* (Broadman & Holman Publishers, 2000), 305.
5. Warren Wiersbe, *The Bible Exposition Commentary,* vol. 2 (Victor Books, 1996), 253.

Week Seven: Commitment

1. David L. Woodall, "2 Corinthians," in *The Moody Bible Commentary*, ed. Michael A. Rydelnik and Michael Vanlaningham (Moody Publishers, 2014), 1814.
2. John Piper, *Don't Waste Your Life* (Crossway: 2003), 47.
3. Mary DeMuth, *Jesus Every Day* (Harvest House, 2018), 317.
4. Barton, et al., *Life Application Bible Commentary,* 220.
5. Williams, *Opening Up 2 Timothy*, 96.
6. DeMuth, *Jesus Every Day*, 326.
7. Radmacher, et al., *Nelson's New Illustrated Bible Commentary,* 1617.
8. Oswald Chambers, *My Utmost for His Highest Updated Edition*, Feb. 6.

Week Eight: Steadfastness

1. Cleere Cherry, *Be Still: 90 Devotions for the Hopeful Heart* (Dayspring, 2019), 131.
2. MacDonald, *Believer's Bible Commentary,* 2126.
3. Bailey et al., *Nelson's New Testament Survey,* 487.
4. Duane Litfin, "2 Timothy," in *The Bible Knowledge Commentary: An Exposition of the Scriptures*, ed. J. F. Walvoord and R. B. Zuck, vol. 2 (Victor Books, 1985), 760.
5. Wolgemuth, *The Quiet Place*, June 5.
6. Wiersbe, *The Bible Exposition Commentary*, 258.

Leader's Guide

1. Wiersbe, *The Bible Exposition Commentary*, 241.
2. John M. Koessler, "2 Timothy," in *The Moody Bible Commentary*, ed. Michael A. Rydelnik and Michael Vanlaningham (Moody Publishers, 2014), 1907.
3. Wiersbe, *The Bible Exposition Commentary*, 250.